Practical Stock and Inventory Techniques That Cut Costs And Improve Profits

C. Louis Hohenstein

 VAN NOSTRAND REINHOLD COMPANY
NEW YORK   CINCINNATI   TORONTO   LONDON   MELBOURNE

Copyright © 1982 by Van Nostrand Reinhold Company Inc.

Library of Congress Catalog Card Number: 81-23972
ISBN: 0-442-23609-3

Manufactured in the United States of America

Published by Van Nostrand Reinhold Company Inc.
135 West 50th Street, New York, N.Y. 10020

Van Nostrand Reinhold Publishing
1410 Birchmount Road
Scarborough, Ontario MIP 2E7, Canada

Van Nostrand Reinhold Australia Pty. Ltd.
17 Queen Street
Mitcham, Victoria 3132, Australia

Van Nostrand Reinhold Company Limited
Molly Millars Lane
Wokingham, Berkshire, England

15 14 13 12 11 10 9 8 7 6 5 4 3 2 1

Library of Congress Cataloging in Publication Data

Hohenstein, C. Louis (Charles Louis), 1930-
  Practical stock and inventory techniques that
cut costs and improve profits.

  Includes index.
  1. Inventory control. I. Title.
HD40.H63   658.7'87   81-23972
ISBN 0-442-23609-3   AACR2

Preface

This book is designed to show managers like yourself how to reduce expenses and increase profits with practical stock management.

While there are numerous scientific and technical books on theoretical inventory control, there are relatively few on practical stock management intended for the working manager. And the three practical decisions we must all make are (1) *whether* to buy an item at all and if so, (2) *how much* to buy, and (3) *when* to buy. The purpose of this book, therefore, is to explain in plain language how to find the best answers to these three practical stock-management decisions. The correct answer to these three questions will cut your operating costs.

Although most of this book is based on long-established knowledge about how to optimize inventory (presented in practical terms), some of the material presented in this book is directed to new and current stock-management problems. For example, rising inflation brings more frequent price increases. When a price increase is known in advance, a special buy-ahead opportunity exists. The technique explained in this book shows how to maximize profits during this buy ahead opportunity, while at the same time limiting your risk.

While this book is primarily directed to managers in the millions of business concerns involved with manufacturing, wholesale and retail trade, service industries, and contract construction, managers in governmental and other institutions can equally well use the know-how contained in this book. Additionally, although U. S. dollars are used for the examples given, and decimal monetary unit may be substituted, and the techniques contained in this book will then be useful for application in other countries of the world.

C. Louis Hohenstein

Contents

Practical Stock and Inventory Techniques That Cut Costs And Improve Profits

1. Introduction

Effective stock management is a subject that leads to lower costs and bigger profits—regardless of the size of your business or institution.

To control costs and improve profits, it is necessary to actively manage every asset we own. And it is particularly true of the management of goods and materials we buy and keep on hand either for our own use or for resale. This book shows you how to avoid unnecessary stock costs by skillful stock management.

It is possible to provide virtually perfect stock service to our stock users or customers, but only at a high cost of keeping inventory. Correspondingly, it is possible to substantially cut stock by providing a minimum level of service. On the other hand, if service and stock availability are reduced, sales may be lost, or other cost penalties due to stockouts may accure. (A *stockout* is the common term for the condition of being out of stock for an item.)

Profits can be increased and total costs reduced by effective stock management. Failure to effectively manage your stock of goods and materials can result in increased costs due to excessive on-hand stock, lost profit, or inavailability of stock.

Some of the costs we can avoid by skillful stock management are:

1. Excess on-hand stock that ties up money for stock investment and uses extra storage space. Excess stock usually results from ordering in quantities too large, or stocking unnecessary items.
2. Frequently ordering in small quantities, which increases the number of orders received, handled, shelved, and accounted for.
3. Ordering too late and thereby running out of a needed item.

4. Ordering too early and thereby receiving a new replenishing shipment before it's actually needed, which contributes to excess on-hand stock.

As a practical matter, it isn't possible to be perfect in avoiding the cost penalties of holding stock. Rather, we will attempt to balance the desired service level of stock availability to our customers and users against the cost of holding stock for their use. It is the purpose of this book to help you manage, in a practical way, and feasibly reduce total stock costs while providing an optimum service level.

You may hear the subject of stock management also called *inventory control*. *Inventory* is just a longer word for stock. Inventory control means the same as stock management, but the words *stock management* are more descriptive of what we actually do. The word *stock* includes all types of stock—stocks of items for sale, stocks of supplies for our own use like office supplies, stocks of parts for equipment maintenance, and any item we use ourselves or sell to others.

Effective stock management means providing the desired stock service level or maximizing your profit while at the same time keeping your total stock costs as low as possible by—

1. selecting products that initially sell well, and discontinuing those that stop selling;
2. purchasing the right quantity (how much to buy);
3. purchasing at the right time (when to buy);
4. keeping your total inventory investment in balance with the expected levels of sales or use.

What does it take to do this? Your first decision is *what* to stock (based on your *merchandising decision*, which is based on what your customers want, if you stock for resale, or if not for resale but for your own use, a *supply decision* about what items your users need). In the case of supplies stock in larger firms (as opposed to stock for resale), often the supply decision is made for you when users requisition supply items. Complementing the decision of what to stock is that of what to discontinue stocking when demand for the item falls to a low level.

Your next two decisions are *how much* to buy and, when you get low on stock, *when* to reorder. These three decisions are important because they are the essence of actual stock management. How you arrive at answers to these decisions is also important because the answers determine both your total inventory investment and the individual costs of ordering, handling, and holding goods in stock. As a result, any stock-management system intended to reduce costs is implemented by the decisions: (1) whether or not to stock a given item, (2) how much to order, and (3) when to order.

While the decision of whether to order and stock a specific item is usually made by a responsible business manager, decisions about how much and when to order are sometimes made arbitrarily by clerical or purchasing personnel, and occasionally even by suppliers' sales representatives.

Often, guesswork is used to determine how much and when to buy and this contributes to the unnecessary costs of ordering, handling, and holding inventory. You should know that whoever makes the how-much and when-to-buy decisions for stocked items determines the amount of your inventory investment. These decisions can be made by others you authorize to execute *your* inventory policy if given decision-making guides.

There are several tools you and others can use to help make effective decisions about how much to buy, when to buy, and about how much money to invest in stock at any given time. The rest of this book is devoted to giving you pratical help in deciding how much to order, when to order, and how to manage your stock in the least costly way.

HOW MUCH TO BUY

Let's take the decision of how much to buy. Rather than risking a guess, there's a short formula you may use as a guide. It has a five-dollar name, the *Economic Order Quantity* formula, abbreviated EOQ. With a simple pocket calculator, only a few seconds are needed to figure out how much to order for any product you stock. And of course the formula answer is only a guide. You can actually order any quantity you want if you have reason to do so. For example, if the order quantity guide indicates purchasing a quantity of 20, and the item is normally packaged and sold in dozens, of course buy 24. But the formula will help you to avoid large mistakes. For example, it may indicate an ideal purchase of only 20 of an item, not the 144 the salesperson suggested. In chapter 2 I will show you how to use the Economic Order Quantity formula.

WHEN TO ORDER

In the same way the Economic Order Quantity formula gives you a guide of how much to buy, another easy formula helps you to decide when to order. The time to reorder any item is signaled by a minimum stock level, sometimes simply called a "minimum." But more accurately it is called the *reorder point* and is abbreviated ROP.

Regardless of whether you call this low stock level the minimum or the reorder point, when your on-hand stock gets down to that point, you must send in an order for more. If your reorder point is too high, you will receive your new shipment before you really need it, and you'll have too much stock on hand. If your reorder point is too low, your shipment won't get in on time, and you'll run out of that particular item—possibly losing sales and customer goodwill when goods are stocked for resale. When stock is for your own internal use rather than resale, the cost incurred for running out ranges from mere inconvenience to extreme cost penalties such as stoppage of a mass-production line for lack of a part, or delaying an urgent medical operation because of an out-of-stock surgical necessity.

Of course it's not possible to be perfect, but the reorder point formula is one of the best reorder guides available. It lets you adjust your reorder point as your rate of sales (or use) changes for each stock item, or when there are changes in suppliers' delivery times. And both rate of sales and suppliers' delivery times affect the reorder point you set. If you now have no reorder points at all, the reorder point formula gives you a basis to initially establish them.

At this point, be sure to distinguish between the Economic Order Quantity (EOQ), which helps you decide *how much* to buy, and the Reorder Point (ROP), which indicates *when* to buy. Sometimes its easy to mix them up at first, but you should stop now, if necessary, and make sure you understand the two separate terms, their abbreviations, and the decisions they will help you make.

These two decisions—how much and when to buy—are the two key factors you will use to manage your stock. Figure 1-1 is a graph of how your stock level for an item looks between reorders. With this graph we'll also see how decisions about the how much and when to order affect your stock level over a period of several weeks.

Weeks are shown along the horizontal line at the bottom of the graph. The on-hand quantity of the item you stock is shown on the left vertical line. The units could be *each, packages, cases,* or any other unit, and for now we'll just refer to the quantity as *units.*

Let's say you've decided to stock a certain item. You order 30 of that item initially. When you receive these first 30, your stock

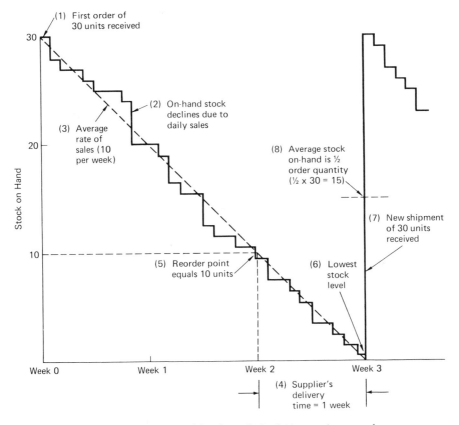

Figure 1-1. Typical profile of stock depletion and re-supply.

level for this item goes from an on-hand quantity of zero to 30. Look at note 1 on the graph. You sell or use several of this item every day, sometimes one, sometimes two. As you sell (or use) these items, your stock quantity on-hand goes down each day (note 2).

On the average, you sell or use 10 units each week as shown by the dotted average sales line (graph note 3). In this example, your average rate of sales (or use) is found by dividing total sales or use (30) by the number of weeks it takes to sell or use this quantity (3 weeks). You obtain an average rate of sales or use of 10 each week (30 divided by 3 equals 10).

Average rate of sales is important because, along with your knowledge of the supplier's delivery time, it helps you decide on the reorder point (ROP). Instead of figuring average rate of sales per week, you could also use rate of sales each day, month, or year if you preferred.

In Figure 1-1 the supplier's delivery time is one week (note 1). To prevent running out of this item, you will reorder before your on-hand stock gets too low. Based on your average sales of 10 each week, and your supplier's average delivery time of 1 week, you would normally expect to sell or use 10 units during the delivery time. Therefore, you would send in an order when your stock gets down to about 10 units, because this is the quantity you'd normally expect to sell or use during the one week delivery time. This is your reorder point (ROP) in this simplified example. On the other hand, if supplier's delivery time were *two* weeks instead of one, then your reorder point would increase to 20 (average sales or use of 10 units each week times average delivery time of 2 weeks equals 20).

The time between your decision to enter a new order for a stock item and its arrival is your *replenishment cycle.* The replenishment cycle is a special time when you are subject to running out of the item and are therefore exposed to being out of stock—a *stockout.* You should also know that the supplier's delivery time is only one time component of your total *replenishment lead time* (also just called *lead time).* Other examples of lead-time components are (1) delays due to the time required to find you are low on a stock item and then to send in a new order, and (2) the time required to receive, check, and shelve a new shipment. As a result, replenishment lead time is the sum of supplier's average delivery lead time plus any internal time required for ordering and receiving. In some instances, the supplier's average delivery time is the overwhelming component of replenishment lead time, and when this is the case, replenishment lead time is the same as supplier's average delivery time, as we will now assume.

Referring back to our original example, if rates of sales (or use) were *exactly* 10 units each week, the supplier's average delivery time were *exactly* one week, then you would know that your *exact* sales or use during the replenishment cycle was 10 units, and your new shipment would arrive just as you used or sold the last one in stock. However, since we're dealing with averages, about half the time sales will be greater than 10 each week and half the time the supplier's delivery time will be longer than one week. Under these conditions you would run out of stock about half the time before your new shipment arrives. In chapter 4, you will see how to set your reorder points to control the percentage of stockouts you would otherwise incur, consistent with the extra cost necessary to prevent the stockouts.

The important point to recognize now is that you must have some idea of the average rate of sales and each supplier's delivery time to set reorder points. Reorder points (or "minimums") cannot be set arbitrarily without running up your stockkeeping costs (excess inventory investment if reorder points are too high, and excess stockouts if too low), nor can they be set once and forgotten. Rather, reorder points must be adjusted from time to time as your rate of sales change for each stock item, or as the supplier's delivery time changes.

Also, a stock clerk with a knowledge of delivery lead time, but without information about the rates of sales for items, cannot correctly set reorder points.

AVERAGE STOCK INVESTMENT

Continuing with the example in Figure 1-1, we'll assume your new shipment arrives about the same time you sell the last unit of stock on hand (note 6). If you again order 30 units, your *maximum* stock on hand occurs when you receive the shipment (note 7). On the *average*, your on-hand stock is halfway between maximum stock (30) and minimum stock (zero in this example), or one-half your order quantity of 30. One-half of 30 is 15 units—your average stock level (note 8).

Why is average stock level of interest? Let's assume these stock units cost you $1.75 each. Your average inventory *investment* for this item is $1.75 times the average stock level (15), or $26.25 for this example. This is the amount of your money that is permanently tied up as stock investment in this item.

Your *total investment* for all stock items is the sum of the average investments for each item. For practical purposes, your total dollar investment is primarily controlled by your *order quantity* decision since order quantity determines the average stock level for each item.

In this example, if you increase your order quantity, let's say to 40 units, your average stock level also increases from 15 to 20 units ($\frac{1}{2}$ X 40), and your permanent investment in stock increases from $26.25 to $35.00 ($1.75 X 20).

Correspondingly, if you reduce your order quantity from 30 to 20 units, the average stock level is only 10 units ($\frac{1}{2}$ X 20), and your permanent investment in stock is lowered to $17.50 instead of the $26.25 invested when you ordered 30 units each time.

In summary, *raising* your order quantity (1) increases dollar investment, and (2) reduces the number of times each year you send in an order. *Reducing* order quantity (1) lowers dollar investment, and (2) increases the number of times each year you send in an order. From this explanation you can see that the amount of your permanent investment in stock is controlled by the order quantity you set.

It is not possible to reduce the order quantity to reduce inventory investment indefinitely because ultimately you would be ordering so frequently that the cost of sending in so many new orders, as well as handling additional stock receipts and shelving new shipments, would be too much.

The Economic Order Quantity (EOQ) method helps you find the order quantity that strikes a balance between ordering too few of an item (resulting in excess ordering and receiving costs), and ordering too much of an item (resulting in greater stock investment and holding costs).

You should note the graph shown in Figure 1-1 is often used in a simplified form to represent stock-management concepts. Figure 1-2

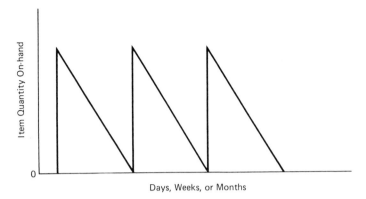

Figure 1-2. Standard profile of stock depletion and re-supply used as a general profile.

shows a simplified profile of stock receipt, sales or use, and replenishment. We will refer to other similar graphs in subsequent chapters.

STOCK-STATUS ACCOUNTING

A stock-status accounting system is a method of keeping records of the stock levels of individual items. Records for items stocked are maintained by (1) recording receipts to inventory (+), (2) withdrawals from inventory resulting from sales or use (–), and (3) calculating the new on-hand balance.

Each piece of information is needed for each stockkeeping unit you control. A stockkeeping unit is each individual item you order and control separately. For instance, soap by itself is not a stockkeeping unit. However, Brand X soap, 12-ounce bars, is a specific stockkeeping unit because it distinguishes this item, which you will order separately, from other brands and sizes of soap. Often it is desirable to assign item codes and thereby number stockkeeping items as described later. Each item of stockkeeping information that follows is kept (or estimated) for each stockkeeping unit.

A typical record card for a written stock-status accounting system is shown as Figure 10-2. In addition to written stock-status records, computer systems are often used for stock-status accounting. Such systems are also often called *perpetual inventory records* because calculated stock levels are "perpetually" available.

Maintaining a stock-status accounting system is relatively costly because each in and out transaction must be recorded. Therefore, the economic justification for a stock-status accounting system must be made carefully. Stock-status accounting is described in more detail in chapters 9 and 14.

It is important to recognize now that the installation of a stock-status accounting system by itself does not constitute stock management or inventory control. Effective stock management or control results only from reasonable decisions on (1) whether to stock each item, (2) how much to order, and (3) when to order. A stock-status accounting system does not make these decisions—only a stock manager does—or the stock manager specifies the rules on which these decisions are made.

However, a stock-status accounting systems is one way of providing information about (1) rate of sales (or use), (2) when stock level is at the reorder point, and (3) if on-hand quantity is sufficient to fill an existing requirement for stock items. Rate of sales and stock levels at the reorder point are both information items used for making stock-management decisions. There are other additional methods of obtaining this same information. For example, a product *sales analysis* will provide the necessary rate-of-sales information. Often, a subjective estimate of rate of sales (or use) is adequate for many products. To signal when stock reaches the reorder point, the bin or shelf reserve technique may be used, both described in chapter 10. In short, while a written stock-status accounting system is often desirable, it does not constitute stock management by itself.

It is more important to establish a correct decision-making method for how much and when to order to achieve effective stock management than it is to only install a stock-status accounting system, whether it be manual or computerized.

You may use many of the formula guides in this book right away with only an inexpensive pocket calculator that adds, subtracts, multiplies, divides, and obtains square roots.

However, because there are many options in buying stock items, many solutions are better obtained by "what if" analysis, where the cost consequences of the decision can be known specifically. Because these calculations are ordinarily time-consuming to make, and sometimes difficult to remember how to make, a small computer or programmable calculator is handy to automatically figure the results of decisions and their costs. Chapter 15 presents methods for figuring answers to some of these problems.

The next chapter explains how to find the economic order quantity for *your* business or institution, to help you with basic ordering.

2. How Much To Order

How much of an item you order directly affects your operating cost. For example, should you order five of an item you sell or use? Fifty? A hundred? For each stock item there is some order quantity that's least costly—and for businesses, most profitable. The correct quantity is the *economic order quantity*, abbreviated EOQ.

The word *economic* is used because it's the amount of stock that can be ordered without increasing ordering costs by ordering too little (and therefore ordering and receiving shipments more frequently), while also reducing *holding* costs by not ordering too much (tieing up more money in inventory and using additional storage space).

It's easy to understand that your total cost will increase if you order too much or too little of a stock item. For example, assume that you sell or use five packages of an item each day, and your cost is $25 for each package. The item could be anything, we'll call it Product X. In the following example, I'll use the term *packages* for the standard unit, because this is easy to visualize. We could just as well use each, sets, cases, drums, or kits, or any other unit of measure. You can substitute the unit of measure that you actually sell or use.

On a yearly basis, if you sell or use 5 packages each day, as we assumed above, that is equivalent to sales or use of 1,300 packages yearly, at a total yearly cost of $32,500 (1,300 packages × $25 each). You certainly don't want to buy one day's supply at a time. On the other hand, you don't want to buy a year's supply all at once either.

The ordering cost of buying one day's supply at a time includes the time and money spent on sending in 260 individual orders each year, receiving 260 separate daily shipments of 5 packages, and writing the necessary receiving and accounting records.

If you order all 1,300 packages at one time—a year's supply—you'd cut annual orders and stock receipts to one for the entire year, reducing your ordering costs, but you'd tie up $32,500 initially for stock investment, along with the cost of space needed to store the 1,300 packages you initially received. The order quantity answer that's least expensive and therefore most profitable lies somewhere between these two extremes. Your total cost for buying and holding each stock item is illustrated in Figure 2-1. This graph shows that Inventory costs per item are lowest when ordering between the extremes of too low a quantity and too great a quantity.

How do you find out the optimum quantity to order, which minimizes total inventory costs? There's a formula you can use as an excellent guide. This formula shows you the order quantity that produces the lowest cost, just as if you'd figured the cost of each order quantity and plotted a graph like that shown in Figure 2-1, using the cost figures for your own business or institution and the costs of a specific item you stock.

Figure 2-1. Total inventory and ordering costs reach a minimum amount between ordering a quantity too low, and a quantity too high.

The formula, along with a simple calculator with a square-root key, lets you get quick answers for finding your least costly, and therefore most economic, order quantity.

Here's the basic formula:

Economic Order Quantity (EOQ)

$$= K \sqrt{\frac{\text{Yearly Item Unit Sales or Use}}{\text{Item Unit Cost}}}$$

Don't worry about the square root symbol $\sqrt{}$. That's where the calculator comes in handy. And as you'll see, using the procedure is as easy as 1-2-3.

The term K in the formula is a constant number, usually between 3 and 9, that represents the ordering and holding costs characteristic of your business or institution. We'll discuss how to figure K in more detail later in this chapter, but for now we'll use a K of 6 as a typical value.

So now our formula for economic order quantity is:

$$\text{EOQ} = 6 \sqrt{\frac{\text{Yearly Item Sales or Use}}{\text{Item Unit Cost}}}$$

Let's go back to our previous example. Yearly product sales or use is 1,300 packages. Unit cost is $25 each. We can now put these numbers in the formula and use our calculator to find the economic order quantity.

With the numbers, our formula looks like this:

$$\text{EOQ} = 6 \sqrt{\frac{1{,}300 \text{ packages sold or used yearly}}{\$25 \text{ unit cost for each package}}}$$

We can now use our calculator to figure the following three steps and find the economic order quantity:

Step 1: $\text{EOQ} = 6 \sqrt{\dfrac{1{,}300}{25}}$ Divide 1,300 by 25.
Obtain the answer,
52.

Step 2: EOQ = $6\sqrt{52}$ Punch the square-root
key on the calculator.
Get the answer, 7.21,
as the square root
of 52.

Step 3: EOQ = 6 × 7.21   Multiply 7.21 by the
constant of 6. Get
43.27 and round to
the nearest whole number,
43.

This order quantity of 43 packages is a reasonable order quantity guide that gives you the lowest total ordering and holding inventory costs for this item. Of course, the formula isn't an absolute answer to be followed blindly, but rather a guide to point to the optimum quantity to order. To illustrate this, if the packages in the previous example were shipped in a standard container of 48 packages to a box, then by all means order 48 instead of the 43 indicated by the EOQ calculation. On the other hand, if the supplier's sales representative suggests an order of 100 packages, the EOQ formula tells you this quantity is not economical for you to buy. (As a matter of side interest, in this example you will need yearly sales or use of over 6,000 packages of this item instead of 1,300 to economically justify a single order of 100 packages.)

FINDING THE ECONOMIC ORDER QUANTITY FOR DIFFERING SALES ESTIMATES

Suppose you are not sure you are actually going to sell or use 1,300 packages annually. Maybe it could be as few as 800, or, on the optimistic side, as many as 1,800 packages. What effect will this have on your economic order quantity? We can figure EOQ answers using *both* assumptions to find the effect on the economic order quantity.

Assume low sales or use of 800 packages yearly:

Step 1: $\text{EOQ} = 6 \sqrt{\dfrac{800}{25}}$ Divide 800 by 25.

Step 2: $\text{EOQ} = 6 \sqrt{32}$ Find the square root of 32.

Step 3: $\text{EOQ} = 6 \times 5.66$ Multiply 6 by 5.66, and get 33.96. Round to 34.

Assume high sales or use of 1,800 packages yearly:

Step 1: $\text{EOQ} = 6 \sqrt{\dfrac{1,800}{25}}$ Divide 1,800 by 25.

Step 2: $\text{EOQ} = 6 \sqrt{72}$ Find the square root of 72.

Step 3: $\text{EOQ} = 6 \times 8.49$ Multiply 6 by 8.49, and get 50.94. Round to 51.

From the answers resulting from these two assumptions, you can see the order quantity decision doesn't change greatly. Buy about 34 packages each time if you decide to follow the low sales or use estimate, and 51 packages if you follow the high sales or use estimate. If you bought 43 packages each time, based on your original probable estimate, you would still be within a reasonable range of the ideal order quantity.

The reason the economic order quantity doesn't change greatly with these differing sales and use assumptions is because the square root in the formula reduces the impact of changes in actual sales or use on the final economic order quantity answer you obtain.

As a result, exact item sales or use figures are not required, and often good estimates are adequate for many practical uses of the EOQ formula. Certainly an informed estimate of yearly sales or use, along with the EOQ formula to decide how much to order, is superior to deciding how much to order completely by subjective judgment alone. If you estimate sales or use more easily on a weekly (or monthly) basis, multiply your estimate by 52 (or 12) to annualize it for use with the standard EOQ formula.

Actually, the ideal sales or use estimate is the average that occurs while your newly ordered supply lasts in stock—that is, the forecasted sales or use for the next order cycle. Therefore, if possible, use an estimate of your expected upcoming sales, rather than past sales or use.

If you have actual unit sales or use figures available periodically (say monthly), you have the capability to make a more precise forecast of upcoming sales or use. Chapter 11 describes some of the stock forecasting methods you may consider including in your management system.

FIGURING THE EOQ CONSTANT K

Previously we talked about how you could calculate your constant K more precisely. The calculation of this constant includes in the economic order quantity formula the characteristic ordering costs and holding cost rate for your business or institution. Here's what goes into calculating your K value:

$$\text{K for your business or institution} = \sqrt{\frac{2 \times \text{ordering cost per order}}{\text{holding cost rate}}}$$

To calculate your K you'll need to calculate or estimate the average extra ordering and handling cost for sending in a new order. Also, you'll need to calculate or estimate your holding cost rate to keep goods in stock. In chapter 3 you'll see how to figure both of these costs. For now I will describe both cost figures briefly, then illustrate how you can find your own K value.

Let's first discuss your ordering cost. This is the extra cost you incur for preparing and sending in a new order. You will include the extra cost of processing receiving records, plus the cost of extra accounting and check writing, all divided by your total yearly number of individual orders. Your ordering cost could be anything between $2 and $20. We'll use $4 as the order cost in the examples to follow.

Next, we'll estimate your extra annual cost of holding inventory. The annual cost of holding goods in stock in dollars, is divided by your average inventory investment to find your *holding cost rate*.

You will include in holding cost your return on invested capital, insurance costs, average stock pilferage or other loss, and cost of any extra warehouse space. These holding costs typically range from 20% to 30% of average inventory investment. Twenty-five percent is a typical value, which we'll use in this example. In the formula a holding cost rate of 25% is used in decimal form (0.25).

Using these estimates and the formula for your K constant, the K value works out to:

$$K = \sqrt{\frac{2 \times \$4 \text{ (Ordering cost per order)}}{0.25 \text{ (Holding cost rate)}}}$$

$$K = \sqrt{\frac{8}{0.25}} \qquad \text{Divide 8 by 0.25 and get:}$$

$$K = \sqrt{32} \qquad \text{Find the square root of 32 and get:}$$

$$K = 5.7$$

Absolute accuracy in estimating these costs is encouraged, but is not essential since any cost error in figuring K is also reduced by the square root of the cost.

For example, look at Table 2-1, a set of precalculated K values for several typical ranges of ordering and holding costs. Look in the column for a 25% holding cost rate, and the row for an ordering cost of $4.00. The K is 5.7, just as we previously calculated. Now look

Table 2-1. K Values for Selected Combinations of Stock Ordering and Holding Costs.

ORDERING COST PER ITEM ORDERED	ANNUAL HOLDING COST RATE (AS % OF AVERAGE INVENTORY)								
	16%	18%	20%	21%	22%	23%	24%	25%	30%
$0.50	2.5	2.4	2.2	2.2	2.1	2.1	2.0	2.0	1.8
1.00	3.5	3.3	3.2	3.1	3.0	2.9	2.9	2.8	2.6
2.00	5.0	4.7	4.5	4.4	4.3	4.2	4.1	4.0	3.7
3.00	6.1	5.8	5.5	5.3	5.2	5.1	5.0	4.9	4.5
4.00	7.1	6.7	6.3	6.2	6.0	5.9	5.8	5.7	5.2
5.00	7.9	7.5	7.1	6.9	6.7	6.6	6.5	6.3	5.8

in this same column, but for the row for ordering cost $5.00, and you will see the K is 6.3. From this you can see that for a relatively large change in ordering cost (or a change in holding cost rate), there is a relatively small change in the K multiplier.

PRACTICAL ALTERNATIVES FOR CALCULATING THE ECONOMIC ORDER QUANTITY

Four-Function Calculator.   A Calculator with a square-root key permits the direct calculation of the EOQ with your K multiplier and the formulas given above.   This is the simplest and quickest method of implementing the EOQ formula for your business or institution.

Stored Program Computer or Calculator.   In addition to this manual calculation, a programmable calculator or computer permits automatic calculation of the EOQ after entry of sales or use data, and the unit cost.   Writing a short calculator or computer program for this computation enables a clerk or other person without any knowledge of the formula itself to calculate the EOQ.   This method lets a less-skilled person perform the calculation, but does require more effort initially to write or obtain the formula for the program.

Nomographs.   In addition to calculation by computer or calculator, whether programmable or not, the EOQ may be calculated by a nomograph especially set up for the K multiplier of your business or institution (Figure 2-2, for K of 6).   The advantage of the nomograph calculation is that it permits you to quickly see the range of order quantities that result as you change sales or use estimates.   Some organizations print such ordering nomographs on the reverse side of purchase order file copies to permit a permanent record of the basis used to decide the quantity to order.

Precomputed Tables.   Another practical method for finding EOQs is by precomputed tables of the EOQ.   Figure 2-3 shows a page from the book, *Procurement and Inventory Ordering Tables*.[1]   These tables

---

[1] Jerry Banks and C. Louis Hohenstein, *Procurement and Inventory Ordering Tables* (New York: Pergamon Press, 1977).

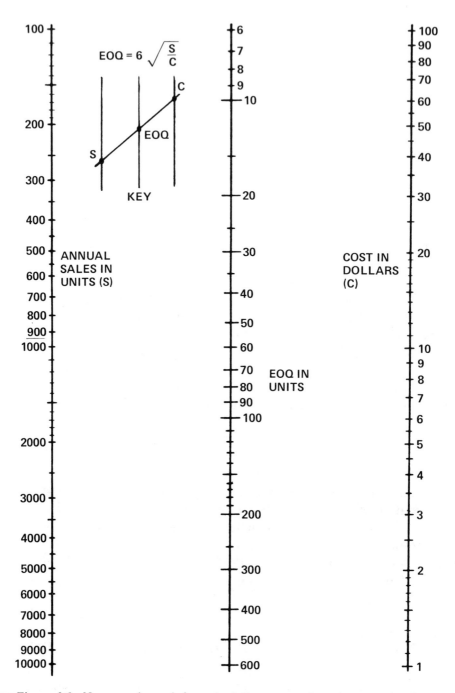

Figure 2-2. Nomograph used for calculating economic order quantity for K equals 6.

enable anyone you assign to look up EOQs, given two table entries (table arguments).

The first argument is your company's K value (computed as previously explained), rounded to a whole number. We'll assume your K is 6. The second argument is the ratio of unit sales per week to the unit cost of the item. For example, assume each week you sell 50 units of an item costing $2 each. Sales-to-cost ratio is therefore 25 (50 ÷ $2). Enter the table shown on Figure 2-2 with the sales-to-cost ratio of 25, and look across the row labeled 25, to the column for a K of 6. Find your EOQ of 104.

PRACTICAL SUGGESTIONS FOR USE OF THE EOQ FORMULA

1. *Quantity Discounts.* This EOQ formula applies to products offered at a single price. If different prices or discounts are offered by your supplier based on quantity purchased, do not use the EOQ formula; use the method described in chapter 6 on how much to order when quantity discounts are offered. The EOQ method described in this chapter applies when products are purchased with single prices regardless of quantity purchased.

2. *Products with seasonal demand.* The EOQ gives you the order quantity independent of the increased or decreased seasonal demand for your stock items. For products *with* seasonal demand, estimate demand during the upcoming season on either a weekly or monthly basis, and multiply by 52 (or 12) to annualize the estimated seasonal demand. Usually the resulting EOQ will be less than the total demand during the upcoming season. However, if the resulting EOQ is greater than the quantity that will be sold or used during the season, then reduce quantity ordered to that solely used during the season.

3. *Stable Price.* The EOQ formula assumes the prices of goods acquired will not change during the time the order is in stock. If the price is expected to increase or decrease, see chapter 6 on how to stock ahead before a known upcoming price increase.

4. *Shelf Life.* If you deal in products that require disposition or use before a specified date (that is, a limited shelf life), there are some conditions in which the shelf life of the item will expire before the last item is sold or used. If the EOQ formula produces an order quantity that will allow on-hand stock to exceed the

ORDER QUANTITY TABLE

MO. SALES TO COST RATIO	INDEX NUMBER				
	3	4	5	6	7
10.0	33	44	55	66	77
10.5	34	45	56	67	79
11.0	34	46	57	69	80
11.5	35	47	59	70	82
12.0	36	48	60	72	84
12.5	37	49	61	73	86
13.0	37	50	62	75	87
13.5	38	51	64	76	89
14.0	39	52	65	78	91
14.5	40	53	66	79	92
15.0	40	54	67	80	94
15.5	41	55	68	82	95
16.0	42	55	69	83	97
16.5	42	56	70	84	98
17.0	43	57	71	86	100
17.5	43	58	72	87	101
18.0	44	59	73	88	103
18.5	45	60	74	89	104
19.0	45	60	75	91	106
19.5	46	61	76	92	107
20.0	46	62	77	93	108
20.5	47	63	78	94	110
21.0	48	63	79	95	111
21.5	48	64	80	96	112
22.0	49	65	81	97	114
22.5	49	66	82	99	115
23.0	50	66	83	100	116
23.5	50	67	84	101	118
24.0	51	68	85	102	119
24.5	51	69	86	103	120
25.0	52	69	87	(104)	121
25.5	52	70	87	105	122
26.0	53	71	88	106	124
26.5	53	71	89	107	125
27.0	54	72	90	108	126

Figure 2-3. Example of order quantity determination by precalculated table.

ORDER QUANTITY TABLE

INDEX NUMBER					MO. SALES TO COST RATIO
8	9	10	11	13	
88	99	110	120	142	10.0
90	101	112	123	146	10.5
92	103	115	126	149	11.0
94	106	117	129	153	11.5
96	108	120	132	156	12.0
98	110	122	135	159	12.5
100	112	125	137	162	13.0
102	115	127	140	165	13.5
104	117	130	143	168	14.0
106	119	132	145	171	14.5
107	121	134	148	174	15.0
109	123	136	150	177	15.5
111	125	139	152	180	16.0
113	127	141	155	183	16.5
114	129	143	157	186	17.0
116	130	145	159	188	17.5
118	132	147	162	191	18.0
119	134	149	164	194	18.5
121	136	151	166	196	19.0
122	138	153	168	199	19.5
124	139	155	170	201	20.0
125	141	157	173	204	20.5
127	143	159	175	206	21.0
128	145	161	177	209	21.5
130	146	162	179	211	22.0
131	148	164	181	214	22.5
133	150	166	183	216	23.0
134	151	168	185	218	23.5
136	153	170	187	221	24.0
137	154	171	189	223	24.5
139	156	173	191	225	25.0
140	157	175	192	227	25.5
141	159	177	194	230	26.0
143	160	178	196	232	26.5
144	162	180	198	234	27.0

Figure 2-3. (Continued).

shelf life at the expected rate of sales, reduce the quantity ordered so that on-hand stock will not exceed shelf life.

5. *Ordering multiple items at one time.* This EOQ formula is based
on your ability to send in a single order for an item at any time.
If you *must* send in a group of orders at once (to qualify for a
total order discount for example, or because a supplier will accept only a minimum order, or for any other reason), then this
type of ordering is a *line buy.* For an explanation of the line-buy
order procedure, see chapter 7.

STEPS FOR USING THE EOQ FORMULA

1. *Find or Estimate Your Ordering Cost.* Read chapter 3 on calculating ordering costs. Until you do calculate your ordering cost,
you may estimate this cost for preliminary use.

2. *Find or Estimate Your Holding Cost Rate.* Holding cost rate is
also described in chapter 3. While it is desirable to actually calculate holding cost rate, you may similarly estimate it for initial
use.

3. *Determine your K multiplier.* Use the ordering cost and holding
cost rate described above to find your K multiplier. Either calculate it from the formula shown in this chapter, or from Table
2-1.

4. *Decide how you will calculate the EOQ,* that is, whether by
pocket calculator, programmable calculator, computer, nomograph, or other method.

5. *Decide how you will estimate item sales or use for calculating
EOQs.* If a subjective estimate is used, the estimate must be made
by a person who has an actual knowledge of sales activity. Otherwise stock records must be used to estimate or project sales.

6. *Prepare a written procedure* for others to use, including several
typical examples.

7. *Train or show others* who will decide how much to order how to
use this method of determining the EOQ.

8. *Periodically refigure your ordering cost and holding cost rate* (perhaps yearly) to determine if these factors and your K multiplier
have changed.

3. How To Estimate Your Ordering and Holding Costs

In the previous chapter you saw how to use the EOQ formula for deciding how much to buy. The regular EOQ formula minimizes your total inventory cost for *ordering* stock on the one hand, and the cost of *holding* goods in stock on the other. These two opposing costs, which are minimized by the EOQ formula, are based on the extra cost of sending in a new order (ordering cost), and the extra cost of holding more stock in inventory for a period of time (holding cost). Knowing these costs is the key to using the regular EOQ formula for better stock management.

In chapter 2 we assumed you had an extra ordering cost of $4 each time you ordered an item, and a holding cost rate of 25% of your average annual stock investment. This chapter shows you how to calculate or estimate ordering and holding costs for your own business or institution. A close estimate is satisfactory for use; you won't need these costs penny-accurate. You should know that these costs are also used for buying decisions when you're offered quantity discounts, as we'll discuss in chapter 6, and for stocking-ahead decisions before a price increase, which is described in Chapter 7.

The reason for calculating both ordering and holding costs for the EOQ formula is not to *allocate* or to spread the total cost of ordering or holding stock. Rather the purpose is to include in the EOQ formula the *extra cost*, in terms of either time or money, for ordering or holding goods in stock. University economists call these extra costs *marginal costs* or *incremental costs*, but we'll just stick with the words *extra costs*. Therefore, in figuring extra costs of ordering and holding stock, we'll leave out costs that we already have that won't normally go up if we order a larger order quantity (the cost of stockroom space, for example).

Because these extra costs of ordering and holding stock are not regular financial accounting categories, they require a special effort to figure them, and also because they are extra costs, frequently some judgment is required to decide what's an extra cost versus what's a fixed cost, which is *not* extra.

Now let's look at both ordering and holding costs; we'll take ordering costs first.

ORDERING COSTS

Exactly what is ordering cost? It's the time and extra cost required to send in an order for an item, receive it, handle the bill, and pay for it, *regardless of the quantity ordered*. Some people call this the *fixed cost of order acquisition*, but we'll just stick with the words *ordering costs*.

You now need to estimate some annual figures for your business or institution, the more accurate the better, but absolute accuracy isn't required. Also, you may make these estimates for a typical week (or month) and multiply by 52 (or 12) to convert them to yearly figures.

Here's what you need:

1. How many orders for individual items do you send in for a year? If you write a line in a notebook as a memo to yourself every time you need to reorder an item, you could count the total lines and find the number of orders for separate items you send in each year. You could do the same if you used printed purchase orders: Count the number of line items on your purchase orders. Let's assume you average sending 60 orders each month. This is equivalent to 720 orders yearly (60 X 12).
2. Estimate the time and cost required to write and mail purchase orders to your suppliers yearly. (If you do it yourself, as is often the case for owner-managers, estimate the time required and a fair price for your time. I'll come back to the rationale for paying yourself for doing this in a moment.)

3. Estimate the time and cost to receive orders during the year.
4. Estimate the time and cost of bookkeeping you must do for handling bills and sending checks in payment for orders. Also include the cost of all direct supplies you use: checks, postage, purchase order forms if you use them, envelopes, etc.

Don't include any cost of bookkeeping associated with general business activity, because you need to do bookkeeping anyway. An example of this is the cost of preparing income and expense statements, taking physical inventory, or routinely checking display and stockroom shelves for on-hand quantities, which you'd normally do anyhow. These costs don't directly change if you send in one more order, and therefore should not be included.

Now add all the extra costs for ordering from items 2, 3, and 4. Make sure they're all converted to yearly cost. Let's assume your total yearly ordering costs come to $2,850. Next, divide the yearly orders for individual items (720) into total ordering costs ($2,850). Based on our assumed figures, your ordering cost per order is $3.96 ($2,850 divided by the 720 items ordered). This fixed ordering cost represents your ordering cost regardless of whether you order a quantity of 1 or 100 of any item.

Also, it represents the extra cost of sending in one more order. If you do send in an order, you will incur this cost in either the extra time or money spent.

One question frequently asked by people in business for themselves is, "What if I do all the ordering and stockkeeping in my spare time? Should I charge that as an actual cost of ordering?" Yes, you should. In many cases you really could be doing something else productive with your time and it isn't really spare time; you're also entitled to a return on your time spent in your business—just as if you've hired someone else to do it. And if you understate the cost of ordering by leaving out an essential cost ingredient, such as the value of your time used to order stock, the EOQ formula will tell you to order too frequently and you'll end up spending too much time on ordering and receiving. So do include the value of your own time for ordering activities.

Once you find your ordering cost, it usually doesn't change significantly during a year. However, you should recalculate it about once each year.

HOLDING COSTS

Holding cost is the extra cost necessary to hold goods in stock for one year. Holding cost is sometimes also called *carrying cost*. However, we'll continue to use the preferred term *holding cost*.

Whereas ordering cost (as we previously discussed) is the same for each order regardless of quantity ordered, holding cost varies up or down in proportion to the quantity ordered. For example, you may find it costs you $0.20 each year to hold $1 worth of your average stock investment. Therefore to hold $2 worth of average stock, it will cost you $0.40 each year. You can see your actual dollars of holding cost are directly related to the amount of your average stock investment.

What we're really after here is your annual holding cost *rate* per dollar of average inventory held. In this simple example, the holding cost rate is $0.20 divided by $1.00, or 20%. Be sure to make the distinction between holding cost and holding cost rate.

Once you determine your holding cost rate, you can find holding cost dollars for any amount of average inventory.

Now, as an example, let's figure a holding cost rate for a business or institution. First, let's list the cost items that go into holding costs:

1. *The extra cost of money invested in stock.* If the money invested is yours or your organization's, you're entitled to an investment return on any of your own money invested in stock. This is because if it weren't invested in stock you (or your organization) could invest it elsewhere, in a money-market fund, for example, and earn a return on this capital. Since you forgo this opportunity, you are at least entitled to the same return on money invested in goods in your stockroom.

   In setting the rate of return for your own business capital investment, you're also entitled to a higher rate than, say, the current return on treasury bills or most money-market funds. You are entitled to a higher than normal rate because of the element of risk to business capital, directly related to the amount of risk in your business. The rate your bank would charge you for borrowed funds is a good guide. (However, also see discussion of inflation rate on the cost of money in a following section.)

If you do borrow money from a bank or elsewhere to finance your stock, the interest rate charged is your actual cost for the borrowed portion of the capital you invested in stock. In short, this holding cost element is the cost of money. We all know it isn't free.

We'll assume you've got a stock of items worth $250,000, and we'll assume a return of 12% on your investment is reasonable. Therefore, the holding cost resulting from return on capital invested is $30,000 ($250,000 × 0.12).

2. *Property taxes paid on inventory.* Look up your property-tax bill for last year, applicable to stock. The tax bill may also include other property in your business, so you may have to adjust out amounts for nonstock property. Ask your accountant to help with this if necessary. We'll assume your property taxes for last year were $12,000.

3. *Insurance on stock.* Use the premium charged for casualty insurance on stock; ask your insurance agent for this figure if necessary. We'll assume insurance is $10,000.

4. *Stock losses due to stockroom pilferage or other stock-handling damage.* Estimate your stock losses for a year due to these factors. We'll assume your stock loss is $8,000.

5. *Storage space.* Normally you won't include the yearly cost of storage space you already have, because it isn't truly an *extra* cost that increases with a new order. However, if you rent storage space in a warehouse where your cost does in fact go up and down based on the number of square feet used, or if you must rent extra space temporarily because of a large order for seasonal sales storage, then do include the equivalent annual cost of the extra space. Otherwise, don't. We'll assume you don't do any of these and extra storage space cost is zero.

Now adding each of the foregoing individual yearly holding costs, we get a total extra stock holding cost of $60,000 ($30,000 + 12,000 + 10,000 + $8,000). We previously assumed your average inventory investment is $250,000. Therefore, your holding cost rate in this example is 0.240, or 24% ($60,000 ÷ $250,000).

Typically, your holding cost rate stays about the same unless you change the character of your stockroom or warehouse facility or if interest rates change significantly. However, you should recalculate your holding cost rate periodically—perhaps yearly—to see if there's any change.

CALCULATING THE K MULTIPLIER FROM ORDERING COST AND HOLDING COST RATE

From chapter 2 you remember ordering costs and holding cost rate are used to get the K value for the EOQ formula. The K value is obtained from the formula:

$$K = \sqrt{\frac{2 \times \text{ordering cost per order}}{\text{holding cost rate}}}$$

With the ordering and holding cost figures we've just obtained, your index number for use with the EOQ is:

$$K = \sqrt{\frac{2 \times 3.96}{0.240}}$$

$$= \sqrt{33.0}$$

$$= 5.74, \text{ rounded to } 5.7$$

Therefore, your EOQ formula with this K value is:

$$EOQ = 5.7\sqrt{\frac{\text{yearly item sales or use}}{\text{item unit cost}}}$$

Table 2-1 shows the computed K value for several other combinations of ordering costs and holding cost rates, though you may figure yours exactly with the formula given above. From this table, you can see that your ordering and holding costs normally combine to produce a K value between 3 and 6. With your K value based on your actual ordering and holding cost and the EOQ formula, you have an excellent guide for ordering individual stock items. If necessary, get your regular accountant or someone familiar with cost accounting to help you figure ordering costs and holding cost rates.

SECONDARY FUNCTIONS OF THE K VALUE

The primary purpose of the K value is to include your characteristic ordering and holding costs in the EOQ computation. These costs directly balance the opposing ordering and holding costs incurred for stocked items.

But there is also a secondary use of the K multiplier. Since (1) your order quantity for each stock item is a major factor in establishing your average on-hand stock, and therefore your average stock investment, and (2) the K multiplier directly controls the order quantity for all of your stock items, then small changes in the K multiplier up or down may be used to change your overall inventory investment up or down. In this respect, your K multiplier is used like a volume control on a radio, except it's used to increase or decrease total stock investment by turning the K multiplier up or down. The K multiplier is your volume control for total stock investment. You would make stock investment adjustments (increasing or decreasing stock investment across the board) only for some overall policy reason. How and why to change overall stock investment is a matter of business or institutional policy that is described further in chapter 11—Balancing Overall Inventory Investment with Business Sales or Operating Levels.

MISUNDERSTANDINGS ABOUT HOLDING COST RATE AND THE EFFECT OF UNDERSTATING HOLDING COST RATE

There is a tendency for some managers employed in organizations already using the EOQ formula to underestimate or understate holding cost rates. We can speculate on several reasons for this and then, more to the point, look at the consequences of what happens to stock levels and stock investment if holding cost rate *is* understated.

Some managers, when told their holding cost rate is 25%, for example, may misunderstand the calculation basis of holding cost rate, and think the holding cost is 25% of their stock cost. They often insist their holding cost is "not that high, only 16% or 17% at the most."

If holding cost rate *were* a percent of stock cost (it's not), then the holding cost of an item costing $25.00 would be $6.25 ($25 × 0.25) no matter how long the item is held in stock (a day, a month, or a year). Of course, this isn't true. Total holding cost rate is the percent that total holding cost is to total average inventory investment. Thus, for an individual stock item, the item holding cost is a percent (25% in this example) of average inventory. For a stock item costing $25, we would have to know the average stock level of the item to translate holding cost rate for that item to dollars.

For example, if the EOQ for the sample stock item is 43 packages, then average inventory is 21.5 (1/2 × 43) packages (omitting any safety stock for simplicity). Average stock investment is then $537.50 (21.5 × $25), and yearly holding cost is $134.38. If 520 packages are sold or used each year at a cost of $25 per package, total yearly product cost is $13,000 (520 × $25). In this example, holding cost (as a percentage of stock item cost) is only 1% of item cost ($134.38 ÷ $13,000), and not 25%, to illustrate the above typical misunderstanding.

Operating managers should not be permitted to "argue down" the holding cost rate from its correct value if their understanding of holding cost rate is based on the incorrect notion that this rate is a percentage of product cost.

Another reason holding cost rate is sometimes understated is that stock managers may believe it's simply a sign of good management to have all costs thought to be as low as possible. Because there is some latitude in estimating what cost elements are included—and even in estimating the amounts of some of the cost elements (obsolescence, for example)—there may be some pressure to understate the costs.

The consequence of underestimating the holding cost rate for whatever reason, is to increase stock investment above the appropriate level.

You can see why this can happen by looking at Table 2-1. Look at the line for an order cost of $4. Look across this line from left to right. You will see the K multiplier goes *down* as holding cost rate goes *up*. And more importantly, look the other way, right or left, and you will see the K multiplier goes *up* as holding cost rate goes *down*. Although we've looked at the $4 ordering cost line, this same relationship is true at any other ordering cost.

The significance of this is that underestimating holding cost rate acts to increase the K multiplier, which in turn increases the indicated EOQ, and that in turn increases average inventory investment above the level it should be if the correct (higher) holding cost rate were used.

No advantage is gained by artificially reducing the amount shown for holding cost rate, and a cost penalty will result from doing so by increasing stock investment beyond its correct and most profitable level.

SPECIAL ADJUSTMENTS TO THE HOLDING COST RATE

Now that you know the basis of holding cost rate, you should also know of possible reasons to adjust your holding cost rate under special conditions.

Extra Stockroom. Holding cost normally excludes occupancy costs for the space leased or owned for warehouse or stockroom facilities. This is omitted because adding a few more items of stock do not directly cause any additional extra costs. On the other hand, if it is necessary to rent extra stockroom for a special shipment—a Christmas supply, or a large quantity bought in advance to take advantage of a temporary price reduction—and an extra stockroom is in fact needed for that order, then you are justified in increasing the holding cost rate slightly to compensate. This will have the result of reducing the indicated order quantity. This factor will come up again in chapter 5, where we discuss quantity discounts, and in chapter 6, which contains information about buying ahead on a price increase where you are justified in decreasing the quantity ordered based on possible extra stockroom holding cost.

Full Stockroom or Warehouse. Additionally, you are justified in including an allowance for stockroom or warehouse cost if your stock or warehouse space is full. This is because you must make room in your stockroom or warehouse for additional stock ordered by not ordering some other item of stock you normally need or sell in order to make room for the new stock. Therefore, when you have a full stockroom, you are justified in increasing your holding cost rate.

Changes in the Cost of Money. As the rate of return on money increases and decreases due to economic conditions, you should correspondingly increase or decrease this factor of your holding cost. If you borrow money from the bank to finance inventory, this increase and decrease of the cost of money will be directly apparent to you and you should include it in your holding cost currently used. Alternately, if it is *your* money invested in stock you are correspondingly entitled to a higher return on the money, and you should increase this component of holding cost as the cost of capital goes up. The effect will be to reduce your investment in inventory as the cost of money increases.

However, you should know that not everyone agrees the full money rate of interest should be used for economic order quantity calculations during periods of high inflation. The logic is interest rates on paper money, and money equivalents, include points for inflation (say 10%) because the purchasing power of paper dollars is declining at a 10% annual rate. However, when paper money (the buying power of which is declining at the inflation rate) is invested in inventory like auto parts, for example (the price of which is increasing at the inflation rate), the inflation component of the money interest rate doesn't apply to the opportunity cost of capital invested in this appreciating stock, and to that used for determining inventory holding-cost rate. Proponents of this method, therefore, would use a significantly lower capital rate than current rate of return on money. The deciding factor of whether to subtract the current inflation rate from the cost of money used for inventory calculations centers on whether the inventory is, or is not, appreciating at approximately the same rate as inflation. If the characteristics of inventory held are such that they are not appreciating at the same rate as inflation, then no inventory gain is realized through price appreciation of stock held, and the full cost of money, including inflation, can be considered the cost of capital under this condition. However, when the characteristics of stock held are such that there is price appreciation of the inventory, a gain is realized on the inventory price appreciation. In this instance, a reduction in the cost of money proportional to the price appreciation of the inventory can be considered logical.

Product Obsolescence. Product obsolescence is not a factor for many organizations, but for others it is. For example, in the toy industry, certain toys and games can become quickly obsoleted by competitive products, and this factor should be included in the holding cost rate for that industry. You must determine whether obsolescence of products in stock is a factor for you, and include the approximate cost of obsoleted inventory in your holding cost rate.

Other Extra Risks. Possible product obsolescence, as mentioned above, is one form of risk inherent in holding goods in stock. When larger than normal quantities of stock are bought as a result of special supplier deals like quantity discounts, or before a price increase, you may be exposed to other financial risks. For example, demand for the items stocked may drop to less than that expected, resulting in greater than expected holding costs. To compensate for these extra risks, some managers increase the holding cost rate (which includes the rate of return on capital invested in stock) to compensate for these perceived risks. This has the effect of reducing the amount of extra stock bought on such suppliers' deals.

Deterioration. Product deterioration in storage facilities can result from either handling and wear, or possibly from the expiration of the shelf life of the product. If your products are subject to yearly loss as a result of deterioration from any cause, include an allowance for this in your holding cost computations.

Other Extra Costs not Normally an Extra. You must carefully consider if there are any other cost factors that are not normally an extra that might, under certain circumstances, be similar to those above. If there are, you must include a cost estimate of them in computing your holding cost rate.

ROLE OF INDUSTRY ASSOCIATIONS IN COLLECTING MEMBERS COST DATA FOR ORDERING COSTS AND HOLDING COST RATE

Industry associations can render a valuable service to their members by collecting experience data on ordering cost and holding costs their members encounter and compute. By assembling and publishing the average cost incurred, possibly by size or other classification of businesses or institutions within their association, members can study this data and determine whether their own costs are approximately in line with those experienced by others.

4. When To Order To Prevent and Limit Stockouts

One objective in ordering stock is to avoid sales lost (or other cost penalties) because you are out of stock. Another opposing objective is to avoid excess inventory and associated extra holding costs resulting from receiving a new shipment before it's actually needed. This also results in added costs because you have excess inventory.

If you could time reorders exactly, you'd receive your new replenishing shipment just as you sold or issued the last item in stock. Of course, it's not possible to be perfect, but you can aim for minimizing costs by avoiding replenishment of stock either too early or too late. To accomplish this, you need two tools.

One tool is a method that helps you make the when-to-order decision by properly setting your reorder point (ROP) according to your on-hand stock level, which we'll discuss later in this chapter.

The other tool you need is a method that tells you how much stock is actually on hand so you'll know when you're down to the reorder point you've set, a signal that lets you know its time to reorder. Such a signal system can be as simple as (1) looking on the shelf to see how much is left for your important stock items, (2) tagging a box of goods in your stockroom with a reorder card (a *shelf reserve* or two-bin system), (3) keeping a perpetual inventory or a record card, or (4) using computers to account for in-and-out transactions of inventory. (If you happen to have a computerized stock-status accounting system, then it's easy to add the when-to-buy computations shown below to your computer program, and let the computer periodically refigure your reorder points.) Methods for setting up a procedure for stock level signaling are described further in chapter 10.

However, let's discuss how you can set reorder points for items you stock. Figure 1-1 showed you that your reorder point is an on-hand quantity of stock used as a signal for when to send in a new replenishing order. Some people also call this quantity a minimum. When stock gets down to this minimum, an order for more stock is sent. *Minimum and reorder point* (ROP) mean about the same, but reorder point is the correct and more descriptive term.

In setting your reorder point, you want to minimize your total stock costs. If you set your reorder point arbitrarily too high, you order too soon and a new shipment arrives before you've sold or used the last item of existing stock. Your costs are increased because you have excess stock on hand. To illustrate this in a simplified way and extend the same example used in Figure 1-1, let's say your reorder point is 15 packages rather than 10. Figure 4-1 shows the result when you have average sales of 10 packages each week. Your new shipment of 30 packages arrives while you still have 5 packages in

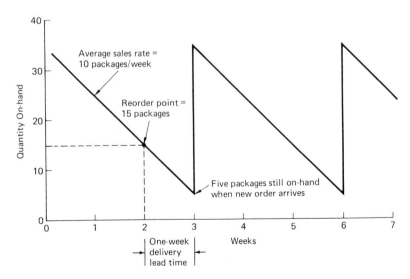

Figure 4-1. Profile of stock depletion and re-supply with reorder point set at 15 packages.

stock. Your new on-hand stock level the day you receive your new shipment is 35 packages instead of 30 because you already have 5 packages on hand.

These extra 5 packages are a *permanent addition* to your average stock level. Average stock level is now 20 packages instead of the original 15 ($\frac{1}{2}$ times the order quantity of 30, plus 5 extra packages, equals 20 packages). As a result, your stock investment, as well as your holding cost, goes up. Clearly you want to avoid setting your reorder point too high.

Let's look at the other extreme, setting the reorder point too low.

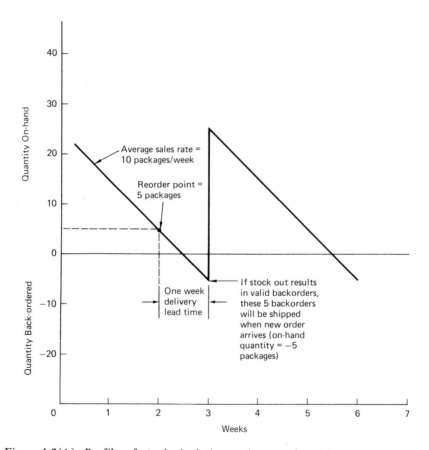

Figure 4-2(A). Profile of stock depletion and re-supply with reorder point set at 5 packages, with stockouts resulting in back orders.

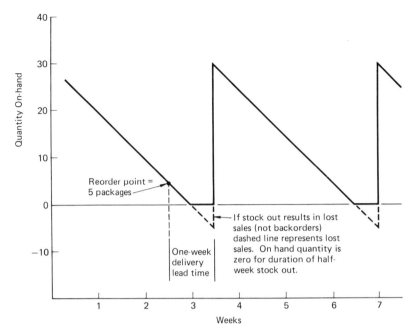

Figure 4-2(B). Profile of stock depletion and re-supply with reorder point set at 5 packages, with stockouts resulting in lost sales.

The result of setting your reorder point too low is that you will run out of the stock item before you get your replenishment. Assume your reorder point is set at 5 packages, then look at Figure 4-2(a). When you have average sales or use of 10 packages each week, you can see you will run out (a stockout) and have no stock on hand for this item for about half a week. For most businesses and institutions, a stockout incurs a penalty from lost sales, inconvenience, and possibly loss of goodwill ("They're always out, let's call XYZ instead").

The size of this stockout penalty can be small or great. For instance, it can be great for an automobile assembly plant that runs out of steering wheels and must shut down the entire plant. How great or small this penalty for stockouts is, determines how hard we try to prevent a stockout or, more specifically, how much extra cost we're willing to take on to prevent the stockout by ordering earlier, through setting the reorder point higher than we would on the average.

A formula for calculating the reorder point to prevent stockouts is:

Reorder Point = Cycle stock + safety stock

Cycle stock is the quantity of a given item that you think you'll sell or use during the average time you think it'll take to get the new order from your supplier.

The formula for cycle stock is:

Cycle stock = Avg. lead time in weeks (L) X avg. weekly sales (S)

Since the amount of cycle stock is based on *average* sales, and *average* lead time, sales can be greater than average sometimes, and lead time can take longer than average. Under these average conditions, you would run out of stock about half the time before you receive your new shipment.

Safety stock is added to cycle stock to set reorder point so that stockouts from greater-than-average sales or longer than expected delivery lead times are prevented. Safety stock therefore reduces the risk of running out of stock before your new order arrives.

Adding safety stock to your cycle stock to find the reorder point has the effect of signaling you to send in a new order earlier. However, *how much* safety stock you specify and, therefore, how much earlier you send in a new order can be carefully controlled by you to achieve a specific *stockout protection level* you decide upon. (*Stockout protection level* is also sometimes called *service level.*)

There are several methods to determine the quantity of safety stock. One practical method is given by the formula:

Safety stock = $1.28 \sqrt{\text{avg. lead time in weeks X avg. weekly sales}}$

The 1.28 in the formula is a stockout protection multiplier to provide about 90% insurance against the occurrence of the stockout during the replenishment cycle. Other multipliers for different stockout protection levels are shown in Table 4-1. In a moment we'll talk about why you would want to use a stockout insurance level other than 90%. But first let's run through an example of the computation.

Table 4-1. Stockout Protection Multipliers To Obtain Selected Stockout
Protection Levels[1]

STOCKOUT PROTECTION LEVEL[1] (%) -1-	STOCKOUT PROTECTION MULTIPLIER -2-
99.9	3.08
99.0	2.33
98.0	2.05
97.0	1.88
96.0	1.75
95.0	1.65
90.0	1.28
80.0	0.84
70.0	0.52
60.0	0.25
50.0	0.00

Note 1: Stockout protection level is also termed service level. Stockout protection level represents the percent of time stockouts are prevented during the stock replenishment cycle.

Assume you sell 10 packages of Product X each week. It takes one week for you to receive a new order from your supplier. You know you'll sell or use 10 packages on the average during the week it usually takes to get an order; this is your cycle stock, the first of the two quantities needed to find reorder point.

To find your safety stock, the second of the two quantities, take the square root of the cycle stock determined above (10 packages), and multiply that by the stockout protection factor (1.28) like this:

Safety stock = $1.28 \sqrt{10}$ Take the square root of 10

Safety stock = 1.28 × 31.6   Multiply 1.28 by 3.16

Safety stock = 4.04, rounded by 4 packages

Add the safety stock of 4 packages to your cycle stock or 10 packages and you get a reorder point of 14 packages. You can also figure reorder point all at once using one formula like this:

Reorder point = Cycle stock + safety stock

Reorder point = Lead time × sales + $1.28 \sqrt{\text{lead time} \times \text{sales}}$

Now we'll put in sales (or use) of 10 packages each week and one week lead time.

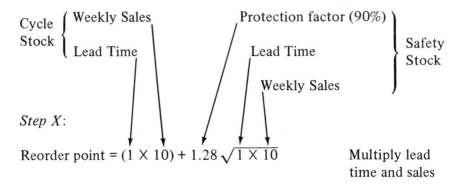

Step X:

Reorder point = (1 × 10) + 1.28 $\sqrt{1 \times 10}$ Multiply lead time and sales

Step Y:

Reorder point = 10 + 1.28 $\sqrt{10}$ Get the square root of 10 and multiply by 1.28

Step Z:

Reorder point = 10 + 4.05 = 14.05

= 14 (rounded)

Add cycle stock and safety stock to find reorder point. Round answer to nearest whole number.

In this example, cycle stock is 10 packages and safety stock is 4. When your supply gets down to 14 packages, reorder from your supplier; you will have Product X in stock about 90% of the time during a reorder. Said another way, out of every ten times you reorder, only during one of these ten replenishment cycles will you actually run out of stock. Figure 4-3 illustrates how safety stock protects you from stockouts.

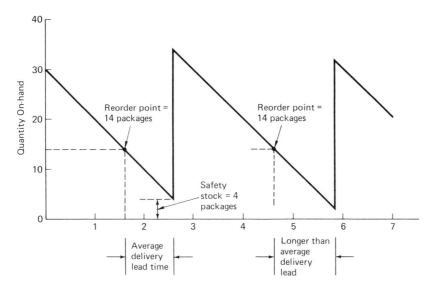

Figure 4-3. Illustration of how reorder point with safety stock protects against stockouts due to longer than average delivery lead time. Correspondingly safety stock also protects against stockouts resulting from changes in average sales or use rate.

You can see from this formula that your reorder point for each stock item depends on (a) your rate of sales or use, and (b) the total lead time necessary to order and receive a new shipment. You need to watch both factors and adjust your reorder point if they change. You can also see that it's undesirable to arbitrarily set a minimum on your inventory records (the same as reorder point), and then never adjust it when changes occur in sales rate (or use) and lead time.

Let's discuss briefly what it cost you to buy this insurance against stockouts by adding safety stock, and therefore what level of protection you can afford. The annual cost to prevent stockouts of an item you stock is your inventory holding costs for the safety stock. This is because the quantity and value of safety stock is a permanent addition to your stock investment. In essence, the cost of stockout insurance, so to speak, is the extra cost of *holding* the quantity of safety stock you've added. In chapter 2 we assumed that yearly holding cost rate ranged between 20% and 30% of average stock investment, and used 25% as a typical figure. In the example just given, safety stock is 4 packages at (let's assume) a cost to you of

$25 per package, or $100 worth of safety stock. Your safety stock holding cost is 25% of $100, or $25. That's the insurance premium you're paying each year to be 90% sure you don't run out of stock *during the period* you are reordering (that is, the replenishment cycle).

New you can ask, "Would I loose $25 each year in profits, inconvenience, goodwill, or other penalties from stockouts on this item?" If the answer is no, reduce the amount of safety stock you specify by reducing the stockout protection multiplier to a lower protection level. If the answer is yes, raise the protection level.

Suppose you want to know the insurance premium for 80% stockout protection instead of 90%. This stockout protection multiplier is 0.84 instead of 1.28. Using the same example, safety stock is equal to 0.84 times 10, or 2.7, which is rounded to 3. The insurance premium for 80% protection is then 25% of the cost of three packages ($75), which equals $18.75 (0.25 X $75).

Is it worth $18.75 to you each year to be 80% sure you won't run out of stock on this item? If not, you can keep reducing the stockout protection multiplier, and thus the safety stock you specify in this computation.

Let's take a quick look at an example where the stock item is very critical and you wish to take a chance of one out of a thousand of running out of stock during the replenishment cycle. With the same conditions as before, what is the reorder point and how much will it cost?

The 99.9% stockout protection multiplier is 3.09 (you will have stock 999 times out of 1,000 during the replenishment period). The reorder point calculation is:

$$\text{Reorder point} = \text{cycle stock} + \text{safety stock}$$

$$\text{Reorder point} = (1 \times 10) + 3.09 \sqrt{1 \times 10}$$

$$\text{Reorder point} = 10 + 9.8$$

$$\text{Reorder point} = 19.8 \text{ rounded to } 20 \text{ packages}$$

The cost of this high level protection is the holding cost of 10 packages of safety stock (rounded from 9.8 packages). At $25 cost per package, extra inventory investment is $250 (10 X $25), and with a holding cost rate of 25%, yearly holding cost of safety stock is $62.50 ($250 X 0.25), the effective yearly insurance premium paid for this level of stockout protection.

In this example I used weeks as the time unit for determining cycle stock and safety stock because weeks is more commonly used. However, you could use any other time unit you chose, days or months, for example.

Let's look at an example using days as the time unit. You sell or use 8 packages of item Z each day. It takes 3 days to get a new order. You want to be 90% sure you don't run out of this stock item. What is the reorder point?

$$\text{Reorder point} = \text{Cycle stock} + \text{safety stock}$$

$$\text{Reorder point} = 3 \times 8 + 1.28 \sqrt{3 \times 8}$$

$$\text{Reorder point} = 24 + 1.28 \sqrt{24}$$

$$\text{Reorder point} = 24 + 6.3$$

$$\text{Reorder point} = 30.3, \text{ rounded to 30 packages}$$

The foregoing is a practical approach to establishing the service level you desire. You should know in summary the underlying theory of the method:

It is desirable for you to keep adding safety stock so long as the extra cost of adding one more unit of safety stock is *less than* the extra cost of the stockout (or stockouts) the extra unit of safety stock prevents.

It is not desirable to add safety stock when the extra cost of adding one more unit of safety stock is *more than* the extra cost of the stockout (or stockouts) the extra unit of safety stock prevents.

It makes no difference whether safety stock is added or not when the extra cost of adding one more unit of safety stock is equal to the extra cost of the stockout. As a practical matter it is difficult to apply this theory directly because of the lack of knowledge of the specific incurred cost of a stockout, and the actual number of stockouts prevented. As a result, the desired service level—or desired stockout protection level (like 90%)—is specified instead.

The previous applied procedure for calculating reorder levels, along with the EOQ procedure presented in chapter 2, is all that's needed for many businesses and institutions. It enables most administrative personnel otherwise untrained in stock management to follow a consistent policy of finding when to order (the reorder point) that *you* decide is best by selecting your desired service level. It also eliminates the need to guess at an inventory "minimum" that's rarely changed when business conditions change.

If your inventory minimums are old, or are set arbitrarily, you may find they specify exorbitantly high and unprofitable safety stock levels for some products, and at the same time, extremely low and also unprofitable safety stock levels for others. You may correct this condition and control your costs with the reorder point procedure described below.

DETERMINING WHEN STOCK LEVEL IS AT THE REORDER POINT

Once you've set a reorder point, you need to know when on-hand stock quantity is at or near that point. For many small stores, simply knowing a reasonable reorder point and periodically checking the shelves for the 20% of stocked items that represent 80% of the value of goods you have in inventory may be sufficient.

Another effective method requiring no specific stock-status record-keeping is the *shelf reserve* system (also called *bin reserve*). A supply of the stock item equal to the reorder point is kept aside in the stockroom (or elsewhere) in a separate container with a depletion notice or card.

The main supply of stock is used first. When the main supply is exhausted, and it's necessary to use the reserve stock, this indicates the on-hand stock quantity has fallen below the reorder point. The depletion notice is sent to the appropriate person as a signal to reorder.

Otherwise you will need a manual or computerized stock-status accounting system to signal when the stock level drops below the reorder point. See chapter 10.

DETERMINING RATES OF SALES (OR USE) AND LEAD TIME

Approximate as they may be, *estimates* of rates of sale (or use), and lead time are frequently used. Do not hesitate to start using a reorder point system based on your estimates of these figures (they're better than no reorder points at all, or those set completely arbitrarily). Lead time is virtually always an estimate unless you have a computerized system programmed to periodically recalculate dates between orders and receipts.

Take care in estimating supplier's delivery time, particularly when relying on sales representative's estimates. In addition to a certain amount of natural optimism about deliveries by suppliers' representatives, delivery time quoted by a supplier is sometimes between *their* receipt of the order and the time of *their* shipment. However the lead time you're interested in is the time it takes to receive an order for a particular item after that item has reached the reorder point (Figure 4-4). Be sure to compensate for the supplier's quoted delivery time based on your different respective definitions, or use your most recent actual experience.

Rate of sales or use per week (or other time period) can be collected from an item sales or use analysis, or from a stock-status accounting system.

Note that inaccuracies in estimating sales or use rates for reorder point calculations have a direct effect in causing a corresponding inaccuracy in figuring cycle stock. This contrasts with the effect of inaccurate sales or use estimates when figuring economic order quantities, where inaccuracies are somewhat diminished by the square root of the sales or use estimate used in the EOQ formula. As a

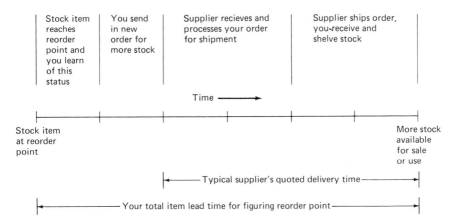

Figure 4-4. Total item lead time is the sum of the total suppliers' quoted delivery time, plus the time necessary for you to detect low stock and issue an order.

result, it is important to recognize the objective of reducing stock costs through more effective management is also achieved by increasing the accuracy of item sales or use figures used for both reorder point and EOQ calculations.

HOW TO CALCULATE YOUR REORDER POINT

Four-Function Calculator. Probably the most practical method of calculating the reorder point, and the quickest to implement, is with an inexpensive four-function calculator with a square-root key, just as we discussed for the EOQ formula. One practical shortcut to the previously shown procedure is possible. In Table 4-1 you saw the stockout protection multiplier selected to provide even-numbered protection levels, 80%, 90%, 95%, etc. The result of this selection produces odd values of the stockout protection multiplier, the numbers actually used in the calculation. For example, 1.28 is the stockout protection multiplier needed to produce 90% stockout protection.

In practice it's not necessary to achieve *exactly* 90% stockout protection because for one reason the choice of this service level is usually judgmental and therefore there is no critical need for exactly 90% protection. Another reason is that you will likely round your calculated reorder point to the nearest whole number.

The calculation with a four-function calculator is made simpler by accepting the nearest reasonable stockout protection level that produces a more convenient stockout protection multiplier to work with when using a four-function calculator. For example, a stockout protection multiplier of 1.0 produces a stockout protection level of 84.13%. Table 4-2 shows, for a range of stockout protection multipliers from 0.0 to 3.0 (selected for convenience in calculation), and the resulting stockout protection levels.

As a result, if one of these stockout protection levels is acceptable, your calculation with a four-function pocket calculator is simplified because the stockout protection multiplier is a round number and therefore simpler to use. The simplest multiplier (though it should not be chosen on the criterion of simplicity alone) is 1.0, producing a stockout protection level of 84.13%.

Stored Program Computer or Programmable Calculator. If you use a computer system, you may program the safety stock computation in the

**Table 4-2. Stock Protection Levels Produced By Selected
Convenient Stockout Protection Multipliers.**

STOCKOUT PROTECTION LEVEL[1] (%) -1-	STOCKOUT PROTECTION MULTIPLIER -2-
99.87	3.0
99.38	2.5
97.72	2.0
93.32	1.5
84.13	1.0
81.59	0.9
78.81	0.8
75.80	0.7
77.57	0.6
69.15	0.5
65.54	0.4
61.79	0.3
57.93	0.2
53.98	0.1
50.00	0.0

[1] Stockout protection level is also termed service level. Stockout protection level represents the percent of time stockouts are prevented during the stock replenishment cycle.

computer reports. See Figure 15-7 in chapter 15 for a sample of a computer report with precomputed reorder points. A programmable calculator will also automatically calculate reorder points when programmed to do so, permitting a clerk without knowledge of the formula to reliably calculate reorder points by only entering rate of sales and lead time.

Nomographs. A nomograph may be used to calculate safety stock, given cycle stock and desired protection level. This is valuable because it permits an immediate "what if" assessment of different cycle stock estimates and protection levels, as well as their effect on resulting safety stock.

Precomputed Safety Stock Tables. Just as precomputed tables are available for the EOQ, comparable tables are also available in the same reference for the reorder point. Figure 4-5 is a portion of a precomputed reorder point table. This table is entered with two arguments.

REORDER POINT SAFETY STOCK TABLE

SALES DURING LEAD TIME	STOCKOUT PROTECTION LEVEL					
	50%	60%	70%	80%	85%	90%
10	10	11	12	13	13	14
11	11	12	13	14	14	15
12	12	13	14	15	16	16
13	13	14	15	16	17	18
14	14	15	16	17	18	19
15	15	16	17	18	19	20
16	16	17	18	19	20	21
17	17	18	19	20	21	22
18	18	19	20	22	22	23
19	19	20	21	23	24	25
20	20	21	22	24	25	26
21	21	22	23	25	26	27
22	22	23	24	26	27	28
23	23	24	26	27	28	29
24	24	25	27	28	29	30
25	25	26	28	29	30	31
26	26	27	29	30	31	33
27	27	28	30	31	32	34
28	28	29	31	32	33	35
29	29	30	32	34	35	36
30	30	31	33	35	36	37
31	31	32	34	36	37	38
32	32	33	35	37	38	39
33	33	34	36	38	39	40
34	34	35	37	39	40	41
35	35	36	38	40	41	43
36	36	38	39	41	42	44
37	37	39	40	42	43	45
38	38	40	41	43	44	46
39	39	41	42	44	45	47
40	40	42	43	45	47	48
41	41	43	44	46	48	49
42	42	44	45	47	49	50
43	43	45	46	49	50	51
44	44	46	47	50	51	53

Figure 4-5. Precalculated table of reorder points.

REORDER POINT SAFETY STOCK TABLE

STOCKOUT PROTECTION LEVEL						SALES DURING LEAD TIME
92.5%	95%	97.5%	99%	99.5%	99.9%	
15	15	16	17	18	20	10
16	16	18	19	20	21	11
17	18	19	20	21	23	12
18	19	20	21	22	24	13
19	20	21	23	24	26	14
21	21	23	24	25	27	15
22	23	24	25	26	28	16
23	24	25	27	28	30	17
24	25	26	28	29	31	18
25	26	28	29	30	32	19
26	27	29	30	32	34	20
28	29	30	32	33	35	21
29	30	31	33	34	36	22
30	31	32	34	35	38	23
31	32	34	35	37	39	24
32	33	35	37	38	40	25
33	34	36	38	39	42	26
34	36	37	39	40	43	27
36	37	38	40	42	44	28
37	38	40	42	43	46	29
38	39	41	43	44	47	30
39	40	42	44	45	48	31
40	41	43	45	47	49	32
41	42	44	46	48	51	33
42	44	45	48	49	52	34
44	45	47	49	50	53	35
45	46	48	50	51	55	36
46	47	49	51	53	56	37
47	48	50	52	54	57	38
48	49	51	54	55	58	39
49	50	52	55	56	60	40
50	52	54	56	57	61	41
51	53	55	57	59	62	42
52	54	56	58	60	63	43
54	55	57	59	61	64	44

Figure 4-5. Continued.

One argument is sales (or use) during lead time, and the other is desired stockout protection level during the period of the replenishment cycle.

For example, assume you will sell or use 10 packages of an item each week and lead time is 1 week. Sales during lead time is therefore 10 (10 × 1). You desire 90% stockout protection during the replenishment period. Enter the table with your Sales During Lead Time of 10. Look across the row to the column for 90% Stockout Protection Level and find the Reorder Point of 14.

STEPS TO IMPLEMENT THE ROP SYSTEM

1. Decide on the stockout protection level you wish to use for the majority of your stock items. Decide on the stockout protection level you will use for any special item you stock.
2. Decide how you will obtain rates of sale (or use) as well as supplier's lead time.
3. Decide how you will calculate the reorder point.
4. Establish a procedure for calculating the reorder point and train or explain the procedure to other persons who will make the calculation.

TRAINING EMPLOYEES ASSIGNED TO REORDER STOCK

Never permit a clerk or purchasing employee to decide how much or when to buy, without guidelines about how to make these decisions. This is particularly important when the cost penalty to the business or institution for stockouts is significant. Since stockouts can never be one hundred percent eliminated, ultimately one or more stockouts *will* occur. When these high-penalty stockouts do happen, the purchasing employee may directly or indirectly receive some criticism, and possibly worry about job security.

To compensate and avoid future criticism, the employee may raise the reorder point to an abnormally high level. Since additional safety beyond what's actually needed represents additional inventory investment, excessive inventory holding costs result. Since the employee is usually never criticized for excessive inventory holding costs, these high holding costs are not a penalty to the employee (but *are* to the profitability of the company). Increasing reorder points is the natural and logical course of employee action to avoid personal criticism, which *is* a penalty to the employee.

Sometimes when an employee is criticized due to stockouts and no ordering procedure exists, the employee may not understand the cause and effect of order quantity decisions on the one hand, and reorder point decisions on the other. Therefore, instead of raising the reorder point to avoid further stockouts (even to an unreasonably high level), the employee may raise the order quantity instead, resulting in higher average inventory quantity and investment.

While this is not the proper direct correction for reducing stockouts, this does indirectly reduce stockouts since ordering large quantities means less orders per year, and fewer times the stock item is exposed to stockouts during the replenishment time. Or, the employee may raise both the order quantity and the reorder point.

For each of these foregoing incorrect procedures, the business or institution will suffer due to increased inventory costs, while the employee will avoid future criticism. The correction for this is to establish a system and procedure for routine ordering, and in the case of reorder points, changing the stockout protection multiplier as appropriate for critical items. In essence, it is necessary to establish a system for ordering.

OTHER SYSTEMS FOR CALCULATING REORDER POINT

The previous method is the *service level* approach to setting safety stock because we specify a service level we want to achieve, for example, 95% stockout protection. Then we decide if the extra cost of safety stock to achieve this service level seems reasonable.

The service level approach appears to be the most practical one for most businesses and institutions. You should know, however, there are other methods. One of these other methods is based on a *known penalty cost* of a stockout. For example, from an accounting study of lost profit, plus an examination of customers' decline of repeat sales, you find the penalty cost for each stockout of a certain item is $5. As another example you might determine that the cost of stopping a production line is $100,000. Therefore, the penalty cost of a stockout of an item critical to the operation of the production line is also $100,000.

When you do know the actual cost of not having a stock item available, the known penalty cost method enables you to set the reorder point to minimize the total cost of carrying safety stock on the one hand, and the known penalty cost of stockouts on the other. While this produces a theoretically "clean" solution, it is infrequently used because on a practical basis, the cost of not having a stock item is often difficult to find or estimate.

INTENTIONAL STOCKOUTS

Another unusual application of calculating reorder points applies when there is no substantial penalty for stockouts up to a certain level of time for not having stock. This can apply to some noncritical items for which substitutes are acceptable (blue pencils instead of red), or for certain mail order operations ("allow four weeks for delivery") as examples.

Average inventory can be reduced, along with a reduction in the holding cost of inventory by *permitting* stockouts, and not reordering until some level of backorders mount. This technique is explained in chapter 5.

REORDER POINT HIGHER THAN ORDER QUANTITY

There are some unusual circumstances when the reorder point is higher than the order quantity. Stock items for which this can occur are typified by high-cost items with high holding costs, low ordering

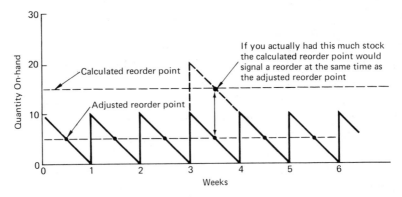

Figure 4-6. Adjusted reorder point is the set when the calculated reorder point is higher than maximum on-hand stock.

costs, long lead times, and high stockout protection level, though all of these characteristics need not occur at once. When these conditions apply, causing a reorder point higher than your order quantity, you may have multiple orders outstanding at one time.

The apparent problem is on-hand quantity never gets up to the quantity of the reorder point, and therefore there's no signal of when to reorder in the traditional sense we've discussed. It is a common misunderstanding that the reorder point must be less than the economic order quantity. This is not the case because the reorder point is simply signaling a time to reorder, and does not specify a quantity that must be on hand.

The practical solution is to subtract your order quantity from the reorder point to find an adjusted reorder point. For example, assume your calculated order quantity is 10 packages and your reorder point works out to 15 packages. Subtract 10 from 15 and find your adjusted point of 5 packages as illustrated in Figure 4-6.

5. When to Order When Shortages and Back Orders are Acceptable More Than 50% of the Time

In the previous chapter we assumed that you desired to prevent stockouts. We looked at stockout protection levels of between 50% and 99.9%, and the required stockout protection multiplier to find the necessary safety stock to add to cycle stock. In this way we found the reorder point that provided a specified level of stockout protection.

Now we will extend the same logic under the condition when stockouts more frequent than 50% of the time are acceptable, that is, when stockout protection levels of 50% *or less* are acceptable. If your operating conditions do not permit stockouts more than 50% of the time, you may skip this chapter and go to chapter 6.

Stockout protection multipliers provide you with a way to set service levels at any point between 50% and 99.9% as we've discussed. At 99.9% stockout protection, for example, you *add* a relatively large quantity of safety stock to cycle stock to find your reorder point. In doing so, you imply that the cost of experiencing a stockout is relatively high, to justify the extra cost of carrying safety stock to prevent a stockout virtually all of the time.

At a stockout protection level of 50%, on the other hand, you add no safety stock to your cycle stock to find the reorder point, and you will experience stockouts about half the time you send in a new order. Because, at a 50% service level, you add no safety stock to cycle stock to establish your reorder point, you imply that the cost of incurring stockouts 50% of the time is nothing–because you spend no money to prevent stockouts at a 50% service level.

From these two extreme conditions of 99.9% and 50% stockout protection, note these three significant points:

1. As stockout protection level is reduced from 99.9% to 50%, safety stock is reduced from a relatively high level to nothing. Correspondingly, the holding cost of safety stock is reduced from a large amount of money to nothing. That is, costs are reduced as safety stock and stockout protection level are also reduced.
2. You may establish stockout protection levels between 99.9% and 50%, and at any service level in between you select, based on a willingness to trade off increased frequency of stockouts for lower holding costs for safety stock.
3. You may additionally lower your stockout protection level below 50% and further reduce holding costs at the expense of stockouts more frequent than 50%, for example, at a stockout protection level of 25% in which stockouts are expected 75% of the time (75% = 100% – 25%).

FINDING STOCKOUT PROTECTION LEVELS FOR LESS THAN 50%

The technique by which this is accomplished is to lower the reorder point below the 50% stockout protection level. For example, if you average selling or using 5 units of a stock item each week, and 2 weeks lead time are required to order and receive a new supply on the average, then your cycle stock is 10 units (5 × 2). Since no safety stock is added to this cycle stock (because it is a 50% stockout protection level) this is also your reorder point for a 50% stockout protection level.

If you now decide to lower your reorder point to below 10 units, to 8 units for example, you will average stockouts more than 50% of the replenishment cycles. Also, you will have reduced your average inventory by 2 units. Therefore, your annual holding costs for carrying these 2 units will also be reduced.

To minimize your costs, you would only take this action if the penalty cost of incurring stockouts is *less than* the annual extra holding costs of the two units in this example. You would not take this action when your estimated annual holding costs of incurring stockouts is *more than* the annual holding cost of the two units in this example.

When is the cost of a stockout relatively low or zero?

1. When an adequate substitute item is available during the out-of-stock duration, for example, when a supply of number 3 pencils is available and acceptable, but number 2 pencils are unavailable.
2. When the supply of items is not critical to buyers or users, or when buyers or users are willing to wait for delivery, as in the office supplies stockroom of a business or institution.
3. When orders are in hand, and some reasonable delay in order filling is acceptable or expected, as in mail-order sales.

In each of these instances, permitting stockouts will lower annual stock holding costs. Stockouts are permitted by lowering the reorder point even below the 50% stockout protection level.

Two criteria for setting reorder points are (1) service level (in which the stockout protection level is specified), and (2) the average length of time (in days or weeks) a user is reasonably expected to wait for the new supply to be received after originally ordered.

In each of the three instances of stock delays mentioned above as examples (when the stockout cost is considered low or zero), the cost of the stockout is not low indefinitely, but begins to rise after a reasonable delay expires. Examples of this are canceled mail orders, increased merchandise returns for late-shipped orders, and items not critical when delayed for one week become critical for longer delays. As a result, the average length of the expected stockout is likely a better criterion for permitting intentional stockouts at less than the 50% stockout protection level. However, we will look at the *service level approach* first because it is a familiar concept, and then the *stockout duration approach.*

SERVICE LEVEL APPROACH TO STOCKOUT PROTECTION LEVELS BELOW 50%

You recall that to obtain an 80% stockout protection level, for example (50% plus 30%), we added safety stock to cycle stock to achieve the 80% stockout protection level. Correspondingly, to obtain a stockout protection level of 20% (50% - 30%) we subtract the same amount of safety stock from cycle stock. Of course this stock is no longer "safety stock" in the sense that it protects against stockouts, but rather is "unsafety" stock since it assures we will have an item in stock only 20% of the time during a replenishment cycle. (And correspondingly it assures we won't have the item in stock 80% of the time.)

In effect, this is reverse or negative safety stock because it is subtracted from cycle stock. From now on, I will call it *reverse safety stock*. The same formula for a reorder point previously shown in chapter 4 is used. However, the sign of the stockout protection multiplier changes from plus to minus to cause the subtraction to occur arithmetically, and therefore changes the safety stock to reverse safety stock.

Therefore, using the reverse safety stock formula, the reorder point for stockout protection levels of less than 50% (10% in the following example) is calculated in this way:

Reorder point = [Cycle Stock] + [Reverse Safety Stock]

Reorder point = [Lead Time (L) $\times$ Sales (S)] + [$-1.28\sqrt{LS}$]

To find the reorder point, both cycle stock and reverse safety stock are calculated exactly as shown in chapter 4, except, as we've noted, safety stock is subtracted from cycle stock rather than added as a result of the negative stockout protection multiplier (-1.28). This multiplier will cause (rather than prevent) stockouts to occur about 90% of the time. Said another way, the multiplier prevents stockouts about 10% of the time (100% - 90%). When used to cause stockouts more than 50% of the time, this multiplier is called the *stockout cause multiplier*.

Other multipliers that will cause stockouts at other than 90% of the time are shown in tables 5-1 and 5-2. (These tables, showing stockout *protection* multipliers, numerically correspond to tables 4-1 and 4-2 in chatper 4, but because the sign is changed, they *cause* rather than prevent stockouts greater than 50% of the time during the replenishment cycle.

Table 5-1. Stockout Cause Multipliers To Cause Selected Stockout Levels.

STOCKOUT LEVEL (%) -1-	STOCKOUT CAUSE MULTIPLIER -2-
99.9	−3.08
99.0	−2.33
98.0	−2.05
97.0	−1.88
96.0	−1.75
95.0	−1.65
90.0	−1.28
80.0	−0.84
70.0	−0.52
60.0	−0.25
50.0	−0.00

Table 5-2. Stockout Levels Produced By Selected Convenient Stockout Cause Multipliers.

STOCKOUT LEVEL (%) -1-	STOCKOUT CAUSE MULTIPLIER -2-
99.87	−3.0
99.38	−2.5
97.72	−2.0
93.32	−1.5
84.13	−1.0
81.59	−0.9
78.81	−0.8
75.80	−0.7
77.57	−0.6
69.15	−0.5
65.54	−0.4
61.79	−0.3
57.93	−0.2
53.98	−0.1
50.00	−0.0

STOCKOUT DURATION APPROACH FOR SELECTING INTENTIONAL STOCKOUT LEVELS

The percent stockout protection level discussed in chapter 4 is a useful basis for establishing service level when you intend to prevent stockouts. However, when you want to cause stockouts more than 50% of the time, a more useful basis for establishing service level is the maximum time you expect to remain out of stock. This is so because often a judgement is made of the maximum time the purchasers or users of stock items will accept a delay. (Later we will discuss how to set service level based on *average* acceptable delay rather than total delay). This approach is based on your judgment of acceptable delay, regardless of whether it's the total or average duration of stockouts.

Finding total time out of stock. We will look at a computation method first, and then the basis for why it works.

Maximum time out of stock is found with the following formula:

Total Time = [Lead Time]

– [Time stock for a given reorder point will last]

The first term in this formula is lead time, as we've previously used it. For example, we would know for a given product the lead time is two weeks. Of course, you could use days or other time units, as appropriate.

The second term (time stock for a given reorder point will last) is found by dividing the reorder point you've set by the rate of sales (or use) you expect. For instance, if the reorder point you've set is 5 packages and you use 5 packages per week, then your supply at a reorder point of 5 packages will last 1 week (5 packages divided by 5 packages sold or used each week). The previous formula can now be written:

$$\text{Total Time Out of Stock} = [\text{Lead Time}] - \frac{\text{Reorder Point}}{\text{Sales per Unit Time}}$$

As an example, use a 3 week lead time, a reorder point of 5 packages, and a sales rate of 5 packages each week (note that lead time and sales rate must use the same time units, weeks in this example). Substituting these in the formula above, we find the total time out of stock as follows:

$$\text{Total Time Out of Stock} = [3 \text{ weeks}] - \frac{5 \text{ Packages}}{5 \text{ Packages/Week}}$$

$$= [3 \text{ weeks}] - [1 \text{ week}]$$

$$= 2 \text{ weeks}$$

Now you may judge if 2 weeks total time out of stock is acceptable for this item, as well as test the out-of-stock duration resulting from other reorder points as well.

Calculating the Reorder Point to Cause a Specified Total Time Out of Stock. If you select a total time you desire to be out of stock for an item, you may calculate the resulting reorder point by rearranging the previous formula as follows:

$$\text{Reorder point} = (\text{Sales per Unit Time})$$

$$\times (\text{Lead Time} - \text{Total Time Out of Stock})$$

Let's take this example: Your rate of sales is 5 units per week. Lead time is 3 weeks. You're willing to be out of stock for 1 week. What reorder point should you set?

$$\text{Reorder Point} = (5) \times (3 - 1)$$

$$\text{Reorder Point} = 5 \times 2$$

$$\text{Reorder Point} = 10 \text{ Packages}$$

Therefore if you order when your stock gets down to 10 packages, you will be out of stock for 1 week.

Basis for Calculating Total Time Out of Stock. Now that we've seen a practical illustration, let's look at the basis for figuring the reorder point based on a specified total time out of stock.

Refer to Figure 5-1a and you will see the standard profile of average stock level where sales rate is 5 units each week. The reorder point of 15 packages equates to the delivery lead time of 3 weeks (there is no safety stock). We assume a new shipment is received just as the last unit is sold or used.

To intentionally cause stockouts, we will set a reorder point of only 5 units. Figure 5-1b shows the stock level profile. We know the time required to obtain a new delivery is 3 weeks, and that our supply of 5 units (the reorder point) will last only 1 week at a sales rate of 5 units each week (reorder point divided by sales rate). Therefore, we may find the total time out of stock by subtracting from lead time, the time our supply of stock at the reorder point will last: (3 weeks – 1 week = 2 weeks).

Two weeks is the total time a person will have to wait for an order placed just as the last unit on hand was issued. This contrasts with the average time the average order is out of stock. That is, the average order is received in the middle of the stockout duration, and therefore the average order will be out of stock only one-half of the total time.

In addition, you may want to know the maximum statistical time the stock will not be available. This maximum statistical time is based on the concept that the maximum time out of stock will vary as the rate of sales or use and the delivery time changes. The follow-

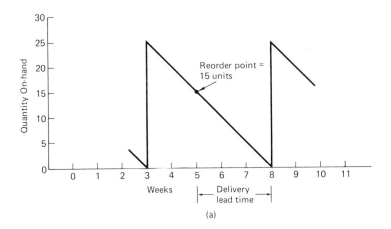

Figure 5-1(A). Stock profile for reorder point of 15 units.

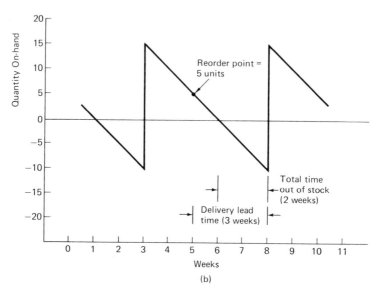

Figure 5-1(B). Profile of stock depletion and re-supply with reorder point set at 5 units. Note total time out of stock is two weeks, and delivery lead time is three weeks.

ing section explains how to find the maximum statistical time you will be out of stock.

Approximating the Maximum Statistical Time Out of Stock. The foregoing procedure provides the total average time out of stock. Because estimates of sales rates and lead time are averages, about half the time you will be out of stock longer than the total time calculated above, based on these average estimates, and about half the time less than the maximum.

Maximum statistical time out of stock is approximated by the formula:

Maximum Time Out of Stock = Total Time Out of Stock

$$+ 1.65 \sqrt{\text{Average Time Out of Stock}}$$

The multiplier, 1.65, in the formula sets the formula to calculate the maximum statistical time out of stock for 95% of the time. To find the approximate maximum statistical time out of stock at other percents of the time (90%, for example), use the same multiplier shown in Table 4-1.

As an example, assume you found you would be out of stock for about 2 weeks at a reorder point you selected. Your maximum statistical time out of stock is approximately 4.3 weeks (2 weeks + 1.65 $\sqrt{2}$ = 4.3 weeks).

Finding Average Back Orders During Total Time Out of Stock. You may also approximate the expected back orders during the average time you expect to be out of stock with the following formula:

$$\text{Back orders} = [(\text{Lead Time}) \times (\text{Sales per Unit Time})]$$
$$- \text{ Reorder Point}$$

For example, assume your lead time is 3 weeks, sales rate is 5 packages, and the reorder point is 5 packages, then you may figure backorders as follows:

$$\text{Back orders} = [(3 \text{ weeks}) \times (5 \text{ packages/week})] - 5$$

$$\text{Back orders} = 15 - 5$$

$$\text{Back orders} = 10 \text{ packages}$$

This example corresponds with Figure 5-1b.

Use of this formula assumes that 100% of the orders placed for the item become valid back orders, and no orders are lost or canceled because an item is out of stock. If you do experience (or estimate) order cancellations, you may still estimate average back orders by finding your back-order rate. Back-order rate is the portion of valid back orders to total orders when you're out of stock. For instance, if you receive 10 orders during a stockout, and typically 7 orders become valid back orders (3 are lost sales), your back order rate is 0.7 (7 ÷ 10). Using the previous example where you experienced 10 orders during time you were out of stock, if your back-order rate is 0.7, then actual back orders during the time out of stock is 7 back orders (0.7 back-order rate multiplied by 10 orders).

Including the back-order rate (BOR) in the previous formula, we have:

Backorders = BOR [(Lead Time) × (Sales Per Unit Time)]

– Reorder Point

You might, through experience, find your back-order rate drops dramatically at some threshold point (because lost sales increase) as your average time out of stock increases, indicating a critical point of acceptability by customers or users for time out of stock.

Zero and Negative Reorder Points. You can see from the previous example it's possible for your reorder point to be either zero or a negative number of units. This section shows you how and why this occurs, and how to set negative reorder points.

Let's look at an example similar to the one we've previously used. You sell 5 packages each week, lead time is 3 weeks, and you are willing to be out of stock for a maximum of 2 weeks. Earlier in this chapter we found your reorder point for these conditions was 5 packages.

To change assumptions, let's now assume you are willing to be out of stock for 3 weeks instead of 2, then your reorder point is:

Reorder Point = (5) × (3 – 3)

Reorder Point = (5) × (0)

Reorder Point = 0

Your reorder point is 0, and therefore when you run out, you will be out of stock for 3 weeks, or the time equivalent to the item's lead time. This condition of a zero reorder point is illustrated in Figure 5-2. This condition is a common occurrence by persons without stock-status accounting systems, or without set reorder points, and who only reorder when they're out of stock. It's easy to see that when a person reorders when out of stock, the reorder point is 0. Consequently they are out of stock for the duration of the lead time necessary to get a new shipment.

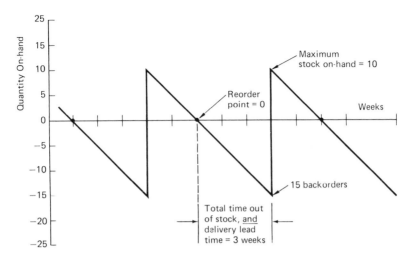

Figure 5-2. Reorder point set at zero. Note that total time out of stock and delivery time both equal three weeks.

In the same way, they could wait a week longer before reordering, and of course would be out of stock not only for the three weeks of delivery lead time, but also for the one week longer they delayed entering an order. This is illustrated in Figure 5-3. In effect, this condition would result from a negative reorder point, as we'll see in a moment.

Negative reorder points have the characteristic of increasing the out-of-stock duration for a time longer than the delivery lead time, and correspondingly will further reduce inventory holding costs, since average on-hand inventory is further reduced. The only occasions in which a negative reorder point would apply would be when the orders for the items stocked can be filled at a later date, that is, they become back orders.

To illustrate a negative reorder point, we will use the previous assumptions (5 packages sold each week and 3 weeks delivery lead time), with the exception that we're willing to be out of stock 4 weeks instead of 3. Our reorder point is then:

Reorder point = (Sales per unit time)

X (Lead time – Maximum time out of stock)

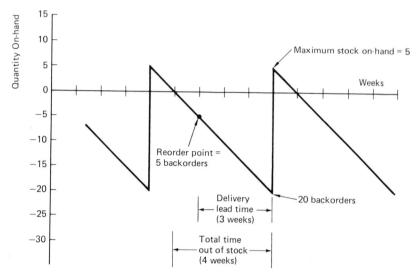

Figure 5-3. Reorder point set at five back orders (or −5 quantity on hand.) Note that total time out of stock is four weeks, and delivery lead time is three weeks.

Reorder point = (5) × (3 − 4)

Reorder point = 5 × (−1)

Reorder point = −5

In this instance you would wait until you had 5 backorders (ROP = −5) before entering a new order as illustrated in Figure 5-3. As mentioned before, with each reduction in reorder point when back orders are permitted, you reduce your average inventory and the associated stock holding cost.

ZERO ON-HAND STOCK

You can see from the preceding formula that as the reorder point is progressively less, reverse safety stock increases, time out of stock also increases, and total average inventory is reduced. When the amount of reverse safety stock increases to a quantity equal to the

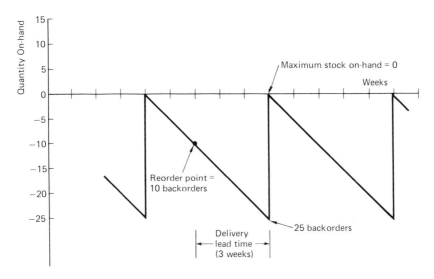

Figure 5-4. Profile of stock depletion and re-supply where no quantity is held on hand. Reorder point is ten back orders (or -10 quantity on hand). Note that total time out of stock is five weeks, and delivery lead time remains as three weeks. On the average a maximum of 25 back orders will occur, and on hand stock is zero.

normal order quantity, average inventory becomes zero (Figure 5-4). That means you've reached the point where you have no on-hand stock (on the average), and therefore no stock holding costs. As soon as a new replenishing order is received, the entire quantity is shipped out to fill back orders.

This special case of intentional back orders is employed by some mail-order firms as well as other organizations to reduce stock holding costs because no shelf inventory is actually held (although the shipping and receiving departments are likely very busy).

When the method of using zero on-hand stock is adopted, the rationale of an economic order quantity disappears because there is no holding cost at all since there is no inventory. As a result, any possible larger quantity (than the otherwise normal economic order quantity) may be ordered and the out-of-stock time increased further. The essential criterion becomes how long you're willing to remain out of stock. You may therefore increase your order quantity to equal the back orders you will have on hand at the time the new shipment is received. For more complex zero on-hand stock systems, you should consult an inventory management specialist for counsel on system design.

6. Quantity Discounts

In chapter 2 we discussed how much to buy based on the economic order quantity formula. The regular economic order quantity formula is used when the stock item is supplied at a single price. Supplier's also offer items for sale with progressive price discounts based on quantity bought, called a *quantity discount price schedule*, or simply *Quantity discounts.*

Let's look at this practical example: You sell or use 10 packages a week of a stock item, let's call it Product X. This is equivalent to 520 packages each year (10 X 52 weeks/year). Your supplier gives you a quantity discount schedule that looks like this:

Table 6-1. Quantity Discount Price Schedule, Item X

PRICE BREAK REFERENCE -1-	QUANTITY		PRICE PER PACKAGE -4-
	FROM -2-	TO -3-	
A	1	24	$25.00
B	25	49	23.00
C	50	99	22.50
D	100	199	21.50
E	200	299	21.25

Because the item price changes from one alternative order quantity to another, the regular economic order quantity method doesn't apply to finding the least costly quantity to order. Instead, use the quantity discount procedure described in this chapter to find your least costly order quantity.

QUANTITY DISCOUNT ANALYSIS

Product PRODUCT X	Unit PACKAGE	Annual Sales 520	Cost to Order $ 4.00	Holding Cost Rate 25% = 0.25

	SUPPLIER'S DISCOUNT			INVENTORY COST				
	QUANTITY		Unit Price -3-	PRODUCT COST Annual Sales X Unit Price -4-	ORDERING COST (Annual Sales ÷ Order Qty) X Cost to Order -5-	HOLDING COST ½ Order Qty X Unit Cost X Holding Cost Rate -6-	TOTAL YEARLY COST (COL 4 + 5 + 6) -7-	BEST BUY -8-
	From -1-	To -2-						
A	1	(24)	25.00	13,000	86.67	75.00	13,161.67	
B	(25)	49	23.00	11,960	83.20	71.88	12,115.08	
C	(50)	99	22.50	11,700	41.60	140.63	11,882.23	
D	(100)	199	21.50	11,180	20.80	268.75	11,469.55	✓
E	(200)	299	21.25	11,050	10.40	531.25	11,591.65	

C. L. Hohenstein and Assoc 1175 Peachtree St NE Atlanta Ga 30361

Figure 6-1. Quantity discount analysis form. Circled quantities are analysis quantities as described in text.

We'll assume, for this example, your ordering cost is $4 for each order, and your holding cost rate is 25%, the same as we used before in chapter 2.

I'll run through the practical procedure first, and then summarize how the method works in a few simple steps. For each price break, we will find your total yearly cost for Product X. Then we'll pick the price break with the lowest total yearly cost as your best buy. This total yearly cost consists of three cost elements:

1. Yearly product cost
2. Yearly ordering cost
3. Yearly holding cost

The Quantity Discount Analysis Form shown in Figure 6-1 is a convenient worksheet for working out your total yearly cost, made up of the three cost items above. Now let's look at each cost item one at a time.

PRODUCT COST

Yearly product cost is how much it costs you to buy Product X each year. Calculate it by multiplying the quantity you sell or use each year (520 packages in this example), by the cost for each unit ($25 each for price break A; and $23.00 each for price break B, etc.). Your yearly product cost for price break A then is $13,000 (520 packages per year times $25.00 per case). For price break B it's $11,960 (520 packages per year times $23.00 per package).

In Summary, calculate annual product cost this way:

Product Cost = Annual Sales X Unit Cost

Product Cost = 520 packages X $25 per package

Product Cost = $13,000

On the Quantity Discount Analysis Form (Figure 6-1), a product cost of $13,000 is shown in column four of line A. For convenience, the product cost formula is shown at the top of column 4 on the form.

ORDERING COST

Your yearly ordering cost is the amount it cost to place each order ($4 per order), multiplied by the number of orders you send in each year. The number of orders you send in is found by dividing your annual sales (520 packages) by the quantity you expect to order each time. For price break A, we'll assume you order the maximum in this price break, 24 packages. If you buy 520 cases a year, 24 at a time, you'll order almost 22 times during the year (520 cases ÷ 24 packages per order = 21.667 orders).

If it costs you $4 every time you order, then your yearly ordering cost is about 86.67 (21.667 orders each year X $4 each order).

Calculate ordering costs this way:

$$\text{Ordering Cost} = \frac{\text{Annual Sales}}{\text{Order quantity}} \times \text{cost to order}$$

$$\text{Ordering Cost} = \frac{520 \text{ cases}}{24 \text{ cases per order}} \times \$4 \text{ per order}$$

$$\text{Ordering Cost} = 21.667 \text{ orders per year} \times \$4 \text{ per order}$$

$$\text{Ordering Cost} = \$86.67 \text{ per year}$$

On the Quantity Discount Analysis Form shown in Figure 6-1, an ordering cost of $86.67 is shown in column 5 of line A. The ordering cost formula is also shown at the top of column five.

To calculate ordering costs for the rest of the price breaks—B through E— use the *minimum quantity* in the price break as the analysis order quantity. In quantity columns 1 and 2, circle the quantity you use as the analysis order quantity, as shown in Figure 6-1.

HOLDING COST

Your yearly holding cost is the third and last amount we'll need to find. This is the amount of money it costs to store (or hold) the average stock of Product X each year. In this example, your holding cost rate is 25% of your average inventory value.

Now we need to find your average inventory quantity for Product

X. Then we'll multiply average inventory quantity by the cost per package to get average inventory: Then we'll multiply by 25% to get your annual holding cost.

Your average quantity in-stock will be halfway between your maximum inventory level and your minimum inventory level. Your maximum level is the amount you have when you first receive your new order. The maximum will therefore be the amount you order (24 packages each time for price break A; 25 cases for price break B; 50 cases for price break C, etc.). For practical purposes, your minimum inventory quantity is zero. Average inventory is then halfway between your order quantity and 0, or one-half the order quantity.

For price break A, average inventory is 12 packages in stock on the average ($\frac{1}{2} \times$ 24 cases); for price break B, it's 12.5 packages ($\frac{1}{2} \times$ 25); and for price break C, it's 25 packages ($\frac{1}{2} \times$ 50 cases).

Then to find total holding costs, multiply average inventory in packages by unit price (or package price in this example) and multiply by the holding cost rate of 0.25, like this:

For price break A it's $75 (12 packages $\times$ $25.00 per package $\times$ 0.25).

For price break B it's $71.88 (12.5 packages $\times$ $23.00 per package $\times$ 0.25).

For price break C it's $140.63 (25 packages $\times$ $22.50 per package $\times$ 0.25).

The entire formula for holding cost is:

Holding cost = $\frac{1}{2}$ order quantity $\times$ unit cost $\times$ holding cost rate)

Using the example for price break A:

Holding cost = ($\frac{1}{2} \times$ 24 packages) $\times$ ($25 per package) $\times$ (0.25)

Holding cost = $75 per year

On the Quantity Discount Analysis Form in Figure 6-1, a holding cost of $75 for price break A is shown in column 6 of line A.

Now we have the totals for all three costs: Product Cost, Ordering Cost, and Holding Cost. Added together, we get $13,161.67 (13,000 plus 86.67 plus 75.00). This is our *Total Yearly Cost* for this product when ordered in quantities of 24 each time. Write this Total

Yearly Cost on the Quantity Discount Analysis Form on Line A, column 7, just as shown in Figure 6-1.

Use this same method for calculating total yearly cost for each price break shown as a separate line on the Quantity Discount Analysis Form. For this example, total yearly cost is calculated for each price break in Figure 6-1. As the best buy, pick the price break with the lowest total yearly cost. You would pick price break D, between 100 and 199 cases at $21.50 per package.

We used 100 cases as the order quantity in price break D, the minimum we could order. This 100 packages produced the lowest total yearly cost of 11,469.55. Why did we use an analysis order quantity of 100 cases, rather than say 199? They are both in this discount bracket.

The lowest quantity you can buy within a quantity discount bracket is often the best buy. In this example we can see this by looking at the way the ordering costs (in column 5), and holding costs (in column 6) are changing as the purchase quantity is increased (product cost will always stay the same within a price bracket; we'll always buy 520 packages at the same unit price, and therefore the product cost won't change).

If we buy more than 100 cases, say 199, in this example holding costs will go up faster than ordering costs come down. Because of this, buying in quantities in more than 100 will produce a higher total annual inventory cost.

If there is any doubt whether the lowest quantity is best, and you feel that further fine tuning is worth the effort, then use the regular economic order quantity formula to determine the best quantity to buy within a discount bracket.

One or two order quantities will usually result:

1. The calculated order quantity will be less than the minimum quantity in the discount bracket. Since you can't order less than the minimum quantity in the discount bracket and still get the discount price, order the minimum discount quantity that you can buy, 100 in this example. This is the usual condition.
2. The calculated order quantity is actually between 100 and 199 cases (say 136 cases); then order 136 cases each time. This means that you will obtain a still lower price by ordering at that point, midway within the price bracket. This occasionally happens.

CONVERTING SUPPLIER'S DISCOUNT QUOTATIONS TO QUANTITY DISCOUNT PRICES

You will need to know the actual unit price you can buy stock items at for entry to column 3 (Unit Price) of the Quantity Discount Analysis Form. Suppliers don't always state prices exactly in this format. This section shows you how to convert from *percent discount quotation* format and *total price* format, to the standard unit price format we use for analysis of quantity discounts.

Discount from base price quotations . In this form the supplier states a base price (say $25) and percent discounts from the base price for other quantities in this format:

Table 6-2. Quantity Discounts As a Discount From Base Price.

QUANTITY		DISCOUNT %
FROM -1-	TO -2-	-3-
1	24	No Discount (0%)
25	49	Deduct 8% of base price
50	99	Deduct 10% of base price
100	199	Deduct 14% of base price
200	299	Deduct 15% of base price

Since you want the price in dollars, find the dollar amount of the discount as shown below, and subtract discount amount from base price.

Table 6-3. Base Price Discount Converted to Unit Price.

QUANTITY		DISCOUNT(%) -3-	DISCOUNT $ ($25 × COL. 2) -4-	UNIT PRICE ($25 − COL. 3) -5-
FROM -1-	TO -2-			
1	24	0	$0.00 (25 × 0.00)	$25.00 (25 − 0.00)
25	49	8	2.00 (25 × 0.08)	23.00 (25 − 2.00)
50	99	10	2.50 (25 × 0.10)	22.50 (25 − 2.50)
100	199	14	3.50 (25 × 0.14)	21.50 (25 − 3.50)
200	299	15	3.75 (25 × 0.15)	21.25 (25 − 3.75)

As an alternative and faster calculation, you may subtract the discount percent (Column 2) from 100 percent, and multiply the result by the base price to obtain the unit price in one step. For example, for the 50–99 quantity bracket the discount is 10%. Multiply the base price by 90% (100% – 10%) and obtain a unit price of $22.50 directly ($25 × 0.90 = $22.50).

Discount Shown as Total Price. Suppliers also state total price for a quantity in this format:

Table 6-4. Quantity Discounts As A Total Price For Quantity Ordered.

QUANTITY -1-	TOTAL PRICE -2-
1	$ 25
25	575
50	1,125
100	2,150
200	4,250

To convert to unit price, divide the total price by quantity as in Table 6-5.

Table 6-5. Price for Total Quantity Ordered Converted to Unit Price.

QUANTITY -1-	TOTAL PRICE -2-	UNIT PRICE (COL 2 ÷ COL 1) -3-
1	25	$21.00 (25 ÷ 1)
25	575	23.00 (575 ÷ 25)
50	1125	22.50 (1125 ÷ 50)
100	2150	21.50 (2150 ÷ 100)
200	4250	21.25 (4250 ÷ 200)

With a price schedule like this, you may not have the option of buying quantities within a bracket. Normally, you'll use the stated quantities in column 1 above on the Quantity Discount Analysis form.

Extra Benefit from Purchasing a Prescribed Quantity. Another form of quantity discount, often not recognized as a quantity discount, is the offer of a benefit contingent on buying a specified amount of merchandise. For example, an offer to pay freight (of let's say $200) when 100 packages or more are purchased, is a quantity discount. The price schedule looks like this:

Table 6-6. Quantity Discount Created by Vendor's Offer To Pay Freight Above a 100 Unit Purchase Quantity.

QUANTITY -1-	UNIT PRICE -2-	PRICE -3-	FREIGHT -4-	TOTAL COST -5-	NET UNIT COST -6-
43*	$25/pkg.	$1,075	$100	$1,175	$27.32
99	$25/pkg.	2,475	200	2,675	27.02
100 and Up	$25/pkg.	2,500	-0-	2,500	25.00

*Quantity normally purchased at a freight cost of $100.

In this example, the freight allowance constitutes a quantity price break (a unit cost of $25.00 for an order quantity of 100 or more versus $27.02 for an analysis quantity of 99). As illustrated in Figure 6-2, the 100 order quantity is less costly each year by $1,072.48 ($14,405.78 − $13,333.30).

FREE MERCHANDISE DEALS AS QUANTITY DISCOUNTS

Let's look now at how to pick the best deal when free merchandise (or any other benefit translated into equivalent dollars), is linked to a purchase quantity.

As an example, let's take the "free merchandise" deal where we are offered the deal of one package "free" for each 100 packages we buy. (Of course this could be cases, boxes, or each, but we'll use packages as our example unit.) The important point is to recognize this deal as a quantity discount masquerading as free merchandise. It is a quantity discount because we get a "free" package worth about $25 when we buy a specified quantity, in this example 100 packages.

Normally, packages cost us $25 each, therefore 100 packages cost $2,500. However, since we get 101 packages for our $2,500, package cost is $24.75 ($2,500 divided by 101 packages). The supplier gives

QUANTITY DISCOUNT ANALYSIS

Product	Unit	Annual Sales	Cost to Order	Holding Cost Rate
PRODUCT X	PACKAGE	520	$ 4.00	25% = 0.25

SUPPLIER'S DISCOUNT			INVENTORY COST				
QUANTITY		Unit Price	PRODUCT COST	ORDERING COST	HOLDING COST	TOTAL YEARLY COST	BEST BUY
From	To		Annual Sales X Unit Price	(Annual Sales ÷ Order Qty) X Cost to Order	½ Order Qty. X Unit Cost X Holding Cost Rate	(COL 4 + 5 + 6)	
-1-	-2-	-3-	-4-	-5-	-6-	-7-	-8-
㊸		27.32	14,206.40	48.37	146.85	14,401.62	
㊾		27.02	14,050.40	21.01	334.37	14,405.78	
⑩⑩	UP	25.00	13,000.00	20.80	312.50	13,333.30	✓

C. L. Hohenstein and Assoc.
1175 Peachtree St. NE
Atlanta, Ga. 30361

Figure 6-2. Computation of quantity discount condition created by vendor's offer to pay freight above 100 package purchase quantity.

us the same deal for each 100 package lot we buy, so the quantity discount schedule looks like this:

Table 6-7. Quantity Discount Schedule Created By "Free Merchandise" Deal.

QUANTITY		
FROM -1-	TO -2-	UNIT COST -3-
1	43	$25.00
44	99	25.00
100	–	24.75
200	–	24.75
300	–	24.75

We can buy any even multiple of packages in lots of 100. As we found in chapter 1, our nondiscount economic order quantity is 43 cases. The question now is, how much should we buy under this new quantity discount deal?

Figure 6-3 shows the form and computations for this analysis. On reference line A I've shown the calculation for 43 cases (our regular economic order quantity) since that's really the base yearly cost against which we'll compare the 100 package quantity discount (where the cost is effectively $24.75 per package), because of the free merchandise.

In this example, the one-package deal is not a valuable proposition, as illustrated in Figure 6-3, and is more costly than purchasing the regular economic order quantity of 43 cases and ignoring the "deal."

Let's change the example slightly. Assume the deal is 2 free packages if we order 100 packages. Since we get 102 packages for $2,500, the per package cost is $24.51 ($2,500 divided by 102). Figure 6-4 illustrates the result with this changed deal. Buying 100 packages each time with the 2 "free" packages is now a better deal than buying the regular economic order quantity of 43 packages. Your yearly total costs are $110.37 less for this stock item ($13,182.75 minus 13,072.38) and this is the value to you of this revised quantity discount deal.

QUANTITY DISCOUNT ANALYSIS

Product PRODUCT X	Unit PACKAGE	Annual Sales 520	Cost to Order $4.00	Holding Cost Rate 25% = 0.25

SUPPLIER'S DISCOUNT			INVENTORY COST				
QUANTITY		Unit Price	PRODUCT COST	ORDERING COST	HOLDING COST	TOTAL YEARLY COST	BEST BUY
From	To		Annual Sales X Unit Price	(Annual Sales ÷ Order Qty.) X Cost to Order	÷ Order Qty. X Unit Cost X Holding Cost Rate	(COL 4 + 5 + 6)	
-1-	-2-	-3-	-4-	-5-	-6-	-7-	-8-
1	(43)	25.00	13,000	48.37	134.38	13,182.75	✓
44	(99)	25.00	13,000	21.01	309.38	13,330.39	
(100)		24.75	12,870	20.80	309.38	13,200.18	
200	--	24.75					
300	--	24.75					

C. L. Hohenstein and Assoc.
1175 Peachtree St. NE
Atlanta, Ga 30361

Figure 6-3. Quantity discount condition created by vendor's offer of a "free merchandise" deal.

QUANTITY DISCOUNT ANALYSIS

Product PRODUCT X			Unit PACKAGE	Annual Sales 520	Cost to Order $4.00	Holding Cost Rate 25% = 0.25		

SUPPLIER'S DISCOUNT			INVENTORY COST					
QUANTITY		Unit Price	PRODUCT COST	ORDERING COST	HOLDING COST	TOTAL YEARLY COST (COL 4 + 5 + 6)	BEST BUY
From	To		Annual Sales X Unit Price	(Annual Sales ÷ Order Qty) X Cost to Order	½ Order Qty. X Unit Cost X Holding Cost Rate		
-1-	-2-	-3-	-4-	-5-	-6-	-7-	-8-
1	⑷③	25.00	13,000.00	48.37	134.38	13,182.75	
44	⑨⑨	25.00	13,000.00	21.01	309.38	13,330.39	
⑩⑩	--	24.51	12,745.20	20.80	306.38	13,072.38	✓
②⑩⑩	--	24.51	12,745.20	10.40	612.75	13,368.35	

C L Hohenstein and Assoc.
1175 Peachtree St NE
Atlanta Ga 30361

Figure 6-4. Quantity discount condition created by an alternate "free merchandise" deal by vendor. See text.

QUANTITY DISCOUNT DEALS WITH OTHER BENEFITS

In the example above I described a quantity discount deal where the benefit was the same stock item. This made it easy to figure the new per package cost at the quantity break since the stock item was the same. A slightly different approach is used when the benefit is in another form, prepaid freight, or a different merchandise item "free" as examples.

Let's take prepaid freight first because we're already somewhat familiar with it as a quantity discount, and it will help us understand the other benefits tied to a quantity purchased. When you order your regular economic order quantity of 43 packages at $25 for each package, the total product cost is $1075 per order ($25 per package X 43 packages). You also pay freight of $125 for each order, so the real cost to you when the shipment arrives at your stockroom (landed cost) is $1,200 per order ($1075 plus $125), and the *landed unit cost* to you for this stock item is $27.91. At this price your regular economic order quantity works out to 25 packages. We will assume here that freight is the same when you buy an order of 25 packages as it is for buying 43 packages.

Your supplier offers you a deal: "If you buy 100 packages, I'll pay the freight." On a 100 package purchase your landing unit cost drops back to include only the product cost of $25.00. This is a quantity discount deal with a cost break from $27.91 down to $25.00 per package at a 100 package order quantity. Figure 6-5 shows the calculations and the total yearly cost for each. Here are the significant points:

1. Purchasing at your regular economic order quantity of 25 packages (as you normally would if there were no price breaks) at the landed cost of $27.91 per package costs you $14,683.62 each year.
2. Purchasing at the 100 package order quantity at $25.00 landed cost per package costs you $13,333.30 per year, a better deal for you by $1,350.32 each year.
3. There is no benefit resulting from buying more than 100 packages each order, as there is no further cost reduction, and actually total yearly costs increase.

QUANTITY DISCOUNT ANALYSIS

Product PRODUCT X			Unit PACKAGE	Annual Sales 520	Cost to Order $4.00	Holding Cost Rate 25% = 0.25	

SUPPLIER'S DISCOUNT			INVENTORY COST				
QUANTITY		Unit Price	PRODUCT COST	ORDERING COST	HOLDING COST	TOTAL YEARLY COST	BEST BUY
From	To		Annual Sales X Unit Price	(Annual Sales ÷ Order Qty) X Cost to Order	½ Order Qty X Unit Cost X Holding Cost Rate	(COL 4 + 5 + 6)	
-1-	-2-	-3-	-4-	-5-	-6-	-7-	-8-
1	(25)	27.91	14,513.20	83.20	87.22	14,683.62	
26	(99)	27.91	14,513.20	21.01	345.39	14,879.60	
(100)	199	25.00	13,000.00	20.80	312.50	13,333.30	✓
(200)	299	25.00	13,000.00	10.40	625.00	13,635.40	

C L Hohenstein and Assoc
1175 Peachtree St NE
Atlanta Ga 30361

Figure 6-5. Quantity discount condition created by vendor's offer to pay freight.

Now let's discuss a price break in the form of a benefit other than prepaid freight or extra merchandise of the same type as that ordered. Let's say you get two boxes of some other item you stock, or possibly even a personal gift or favor.

You must first estimate the real value of the extra benefit. It makes no difference what the benefit is. For example, assume you get two boxes of something else (from what you ordered) actually worth $75 to you, *if* you buy 100 packages of the original stock item at $25 per package. Here's a way you may analyze this quantity discount deal:

Step 1: Find the total cost of 100 packages at the regular price (100 packages X $25 per package = $2,500 per 100 package order).

Step 2: Deduct the actual value to you of the benefit from the total order cost to find net order cost ($2,500 total order cost – $75 actual benefit = $2,425 net order cost.)

Step 3: Find the net landed unit cost of the stock item. $2,425 net order cost ÷ 100 packages = $24.25 per package.

Step 4: Do the price break analysis with the landed unit cost of the stock item at the price break as calculated above.

Your quantity discount price schedule ready for analysis looks like this:

Table 6-8. Quantity Discount Schedule Created by a Benefit of any Type.

QUANTITY		
FROM -1-	TO -2-	UNIT COST -3-
1	43	$25.00
44	99	25.00
100	199	24.25

If you work this out yourself you will find that buying 100 packages each time is worth $248.82 in extra benefits each year. Of course, you will buy the 100 package lot each order *if* the deal is offered each time. Whenever the deal is not offered, you will drop back and buy your regular economic order quantity of 43 packages.

INCREASE IN HOLDING COST RATE TO COMPENSATE FOR ADDITIONAL RISK OF PURCHASING LARGER QUANTITIES

There is a rationale (also mentioned earlier) that states that your holding cost rate should be slightly higher when purchasing larger order quantities (as with quantity discounts) because you are taking a slightly greater business risk (sales or use level could drop, decreasing the need for the stock item, as an example). If you decide to increase holding cost rate for this reason you may do so. Often it makes no difference in the answer obtained. Figure 6-6 illustrates the previous quantity discount example with a holding cost rate of 30% instead of 25%, 5% more than the normal holding cost rate. Purchasing a quantity of 100 packages at $21.50 is still the best deal.

CALCULATION OF TOTAL YEARLY COST BY PROGRAMMABLE CALCULATOR

If you calculate the best quantity discount only occationally, the form shown plus a simple calculator is adequate. But if you make these calculations more than occasionally, you'll save time and simplify your work by programming total yearly cost on a programmable calculator (or other computer system).

The programmable calculator is particularly useful because of its portability and ready availability. Figure 6-7 shows a printout of the initial data entered, and then the calculations for the same analysis quantities originally shown in Figure 6-1. This calculation was done by a Texas Instruments Model TI 59 calculator with printer. However, other calculators are capable of the same function, particularly the Hewlett-Packard HP 41C with printer (at the time this is written).

WHY IT WORKS

Figure 6-8 shows total yearly inventory cost plotted against order quantities, resulting from a product with no price breaks. You could calculate the total yearly inventory cost for one of your no-price-break products when ordering one at a time two at a time, etc., up to, say, 50 packages ordered each time. Then on graph paper, if you plotted your total yearly inventory cost against the quantity you ordered each time, you'll get a curve like that shown in Figure 6-8.

QUANTITY DISCOUNT ANALYSIS

Product	Unit	Annual Sales	Cost to Order	Holding Cost Rate
PRODUCT X	PACKAGE	520	$4.00	30% = 0.30

	SUPPLIER'S DISCOUNT			INVENTORY COST				
	QUANTITY		Unit Price	PRODUCT COST	ORDERING COST	HOLDING COST	TOTAL	BEST BUY
	From	To		Annual Sales X Unit Price	(Annual Sales ÷ Order Qty) X Cost to Order	½ Order Qty. X Unit Cost X Holding Cost Rate	YEARLY COST (COL 4 + 5 + 6)	
	-1-	-2-	-3-	-4-	-5-	-6-	-7-	-8-
A	1	24	25.00	13,000.00	86.67	90.00	13,176.67	
B	25	49	23.00	11,960.00	83.20	86.25	12,129.45	
C	50	99	22.50	11,700.00	41.60	168.75	11,910.35	
D	100	199	21.50	11,180.00	20.80	322.50	11,523.30	✓
E	200	299	21.25	11,050.00	10.40	637.50	11,697.90	

C. L. Hohenstein and Assoc
1175 Peachtree St. NE
Atlanta Ga 30361

Figure 6-6. Quantity discount analysis corresponding to Figure 6-1, with holding cost rate modified to 30 percent. Changes in holding cost rate as illustrated here often do not change optimum quantity to order.

```
SALES OR USE/WK?
        10.
HOLDING·COST % ?
        25.
ORDERING COST?
        4.00
- - - - - - - - - - - - - - - - - - -
ANALYSIS QTY?
        24.
UNIT COST?
        25.00
ANNUAL COST TO-
      13000.00      BUY
         86.67      ORDR
         75.00      HOLD
      13161.67      *TOT
- - - - - - - - - - - - - - - - - - -
ANALYSIS QTY?
        25.
UNIT COST?
        23.00
ANNUAL COST TO-
      11960.00      BUY
         83.20      ORDR
         71.88      HOLD
      12115.08      *TOT
- - - - - - - - - - - - - - - - - - -
ANALYSIS QTY?
        50.
UNIT COST?
        22.50
ANNUAL COST TO-
      11700.00      BUY
         41.60      ORDR
        140.63      HOLD
      11882.23      *TOT
- - - - - - - - - - - - - - - - - - -
ANALYSIS QTY?
        100.
UNIT COST?
        21.50
ANNUAL COST TO-
      11180.00      BUY
         20.80      ORDR
        268.75      HOLD
      11469.55      *TOT
- - - - - - - - - - - - - - - - - - -
ANALYSIS QTY?
        200.
UNIT COST?
        21.25
ANNUAL COST TO-
      11050.00      BUY
         10.40      ORDR
        531.25      HOLD
      11591.65      *TOT
- - - - - - - - - - - - - - - - - - -
```

Figure 6-7. Quantity discount analysis automatically performed by programmable calculator. This example corresponds to Figure 6-1.

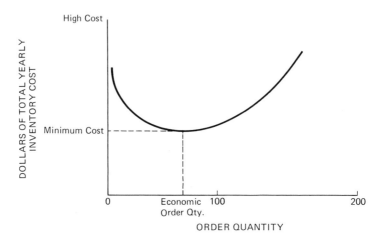

Figure 6-8. Typical inventory cost curve with no quantity discounts.

You want to order at the lowest point on this cost curve because the corresponding order quantity produces the lowest total yearly inventory cost. With no price breaks, you find this lowest total cost by using the economic order quantity formula.

If you sold 520 packages each year costing $25 per package (with no price break), then your economic order quantity is 43 packages as we calculated in chapter 2 for this same example.

But the cost curve is different when there are price breaks. The total cost curve then isn't smooth, as is shown in Figure 6-9. Each of these sawteeth are cost jumps downward, the result of a quantity price break. For products with price breaks, the EOQ formula doesn't directly apply, and you must use the quantity discount analysis described here to find which price break is best.

Is it worth the time to work it out? In our original example at the beginning of the chapter, the total yearly cost of buying 100 packages each time is $11,469.55. If you only bought your regular economic order quantity of 43 packages (but at the bracket discount price of $23.00) your total yearly cost would be $12,132 ($11,960 product cost plus $48.37 ordering cost plus $123.63 holding cost). Your yearly savings is $662.45 by buying 100 packages each time under this quantity discount option.

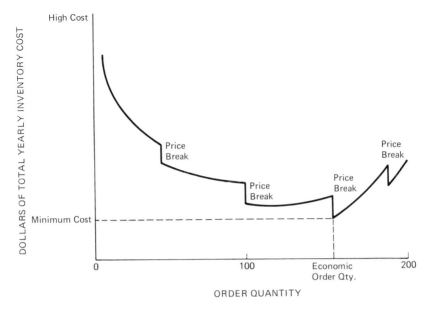

Figure 6-9. Typical inventory cost curve with quantity discounts.

STEPS TO USE THIS METHOD

Let's summarize the procedural steps we've previously described:

Step 1: Copy the supplier's discount schedule for Product X on the Quantity Discount Analysis form. Convert percent discounts, total price quotes, or other quantity price or delivery concessions to the standard unit cost form we use.

Step 2: Use the form as a guide, and calculate your total yearly inventory cost for each price break. Follow the formula guide at the top of each cost column. If you have many calculations of quantity discounts, you may want to set up the calculations on a programmable calculator as described. Find the total yearly cost for each bracket.

Step 3: Pick the price break that produces the lowest total yearly inventory cost.

Step 4: Prove the lowest quantity in the price break with the lowest cost is your best buy either by inspection, or by testing it with the Economic Order Quantity formula.

7. Stock Ahead the Exact Amount Before a Price Increase: How to Find the Economic Buy-Ahead Quantity (EBAQ)

"Due to the continuing increases in the cost of materials and labor, it is necessary for us to increase our prices as of the first of next month."

There's a statement we now hear more and more as a sign of our inflationary times. However you can take a coming price increase and turn it around to make it increase your profits.

The smart thing to do is buy ahead and stock up on the item while the price is lower. The trick is to buy ahead the right quantity.

If you buy too little, you'll forgo savings by having to buy later at a higher price, when you could have bought before the price went up. On the other hand, if you buy too much, your increased inventory holding cost will eat away the amount you saved from buying ahead at the lower price.

How much should you buy ahead? How much is too much, and how much is. too little, is governed by a number of interacting cost factors, and because of the way these cost factors work, it's almost impossible to guess the amount of stock to buy ahead. Also, neither the regular economic order quantity formula nor the quantity discount procedure apply to finding the correct amount of stock ahead when you know of a forthcoming price increase. But the most

profitable buy-ahead quantity may be figured using
arithmetic.

Let's take this example: You stock a product no
(with no quantity discount). Your supplier notifies
increase of 10%, or $2.50 the first of next month.
then be $27.50 for each package as graphically shown in Figure 7-1.
You sell or use about 10 packages each week on the average, equivalent
to 520 packages each year. Your ordering cost is $4 and your
normal holding cost rate is 25%; both figures are those we've used in
previous examples.

You use the standard economic order quantity formula for determining how much to buy for this single-price item, and at the old
price you would normally reorder 26 packages each time. After the
new price goes into effect, you would normally buy quantities of 25
packages each time (the economic order quantity drops because
price is greater). For example, the EOQ is figured this way:

$$EOQ = 5.7 \sqrt{520 \div 27.50}$$

$$EOQ = 24.8, \text{ rounded to 25 packages.}$$

Now, when you find the price is going up, it is more costly and
unprofitable for you to order at your regular order quantity of 26
packages during this special period between old and new prices—or

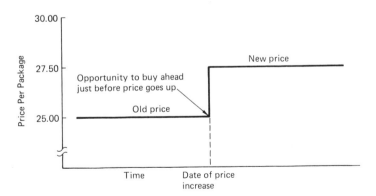

Figure 7-1. Profile of price increase made by vendor, illustrating an opportunity
to buy ahead just before price goes up.

en worse, to skip ordering altogether while you have this special opportunity. I'll show you why shortly.

What is the right quantity to order before the price goes up? You'll reduce costs and maximize profits if you buy ahead 235 packages at the $25 price. You'll earn (or save) an extra $332.00 for this stock item over what you'd earn if you didn't. Just for a little over 5 months, you'd have an extra average inventory investment of $2,937.50. Your effective return on the average stock investment, when you buy ahead this way, is 25%.

How and why did we come up with that order quantity? Let's look at the how, and then later the why.

HOW TO FIND ECONOMIC BUY-AHEAD QUANTITY

Here we're going to do a little easy multiplying and dividing. There are seven multiplications and three divisions, so you'll benefit from a calculator. To simplify the arithmetic, I've divided the buy-ahead formula into three arithmetic terms. After we've worked out each arithmetic term, we'll add the answers to the three terms to find the economic buy-ahead quantity answer.

All of this is shown in Figure 7-2. On the left side I've described each step and the procedure for calculating each term. On the right I've shown the actual calculation using our previous example. It takes less than a minute to work this out. Try it for practice and you should arrive at the same economic buy-ahead quantity of 235.06, rounded to 235 packages. Then you may do the same calculation for any actual product you stock for which you have a known upcoming price increase.

Since we originally assumed you will sell or use 520 packages of this stock item each year, you would buy ahead slightly over 5 months' supply to get your maximum savings of 332.00. If you buy more than 235 packages, your increased inventory holding cost will reduce your savings below $332.00. Alternately, if you buy less that 235 packages, you won't get the full savings either . (However, if you do buy a quantity less than the indicated quantity of 235 packages in this example, while you don't obtain maximum savings, the rate of return on the investment in extra stock is even higher.

If you buy only your regular order quantity of 26 packages before the price increase, you pass up the chance completely to pick up an

FIND TERM 1	EXAMPLE:
Step 1: Take the difference between your old and new prices (27.50 – 25.00) and multiply the difference by annual sales or use (520).	($27.50 – $25.00) × 520 = 1,300
Step 2: Multiply the old price (25.00) by your holding cost rate (0.25).	$25.00 × 0.25 = 6.25
Step 3: Divide the result from (1) by the result from (2) to get the answer (208) for Term 1.	1,300 ÷ 6.25 = 208.0 (Answer, Term 1)

FIND TERM 2	EXAMPLE:
Step 4: Multiply annual sales or use (520) by order cost ($4).	520 × 4 = 2,080
Step 5: Multiply old price ($25) by inventory holding cost rate (0.25), and by the *new* economic order quantity (25).	$25 × 0.25 × 25 = 156.25
Step 6: Divide the result from (4) by the result from (5) to obtain the answer (13.3) for Term 2.	2,080 ÷ 156.25 = 13.31 (Answer, Term 2)

FIND TERM 3	EXAMPLE:
Step 7: Multiply the new order quantity (25) by the new price ($27.50).	25 × $27.50 = 687.50
Step 8: Multiply the number 2 by the old price ($25).	2 × $25 = 50
Step 9: Divide the result from (7), by the result from (8) and get the answer (13.75) for Term 3.	687.5 ÷ 50 = 13.75 (Answer, Term 3)

GET THE BUY-AHEAD QUANTITY:	EXAMPLE:
Step 10: Add the answers for each term and get the economic buy-ahead quantity:	Term 1 + Term 2 + Term 3 208.0 + 13.31 + 13.75 = 235.06 rounded to 235 packages

Figure 7-2. How to calculate economic buy-ahead quantity.

extra $328.16. And for this kind of savings, it's clearly worth it to spend the minute or so necessary to calculate the right amount. Now that we've seen how this method works, let's look at why.

WHY THE ECONOMIC BUY-AHEAD QUANTITY FORMULA WORKS

To see why, we will look at the yearly cost of inventory for several different order quantities we could buy.

As you saw in chapter 6 on quantity discounts, the yearly cost of any item in stock is the sum of the—

1. yearly cost to buy the product;
2. yearly ordering cost; and
3. the yearly holding cost.

Using the example I originally described, let's look at how these costs are figured when we buy an order quantity of 25 packages each time, as we would normally after the new price goes in to effect.

Yearly Cost To Buy. Annual cost to buy the product is the unit cost ($27.50) at the new price multiplied by the yearly quantity you sell or use (520). The yearly cost to buy the stock item at the new price is $14,300 (520 × $27.50).

Yearly Ordering Cost. We assumed it would cost $4 each time a new order was earned.

If you know how many orders you send in each year, that number of orders times $4 will be the yearly ordering cost. How many orders will you send in each year? If you sell or use 520 packages a year, and order 25 packages each time, you will send in 20.8 orders each year (520 divided by 25). Your yearly ordering cost for this item is then $83.20 (20.8 orders × $4 per order).

Yearly Holding Cost. Holding cost is the cost of holding stock after you've acquired it. We assume your annual holding cost rate is 25% of the cost of holding one unit in stock one year. If you order 25 packages each time, your average quantity on hand during the year is halfway between your maximum quantity (about 25) and your minimum (usually zero). This is 12.5 packages. If each package costs

$27.50, your average investment is $343.75 (12.5 times $27.50). And, if your holding cost rate is 25%, the yearly holding cost, to keep an average of 12.5 packages in stock, is $85.94 ($343.75 × 0.25).

Total Yearly Cost. We can now add cost to buy, cost to order, and cost to hold and find total yearly cost to buy, acquire, and hold this stock item. It costs your $14,300 to buy, $83.20 to order, and $85.94 to hold. Therefore, your total yearly stock cost for this item is $14,469.14 *after the new price* becomes effective. If you can buy, order, and hold this product for an amount less than the yearly cost of $14,469.14 by buying ahead, then you reduce your costs and improve profits.

Let's see what the effective yearly cost is for buying another quantity of stock, say 260 packages at the old price, while we still can. Since this analysis quantity is exactly a half-year's supply of the 520 packages we sell or use each year, we'll work out the total cost of buying this stock for a full year, and then reduce it by half because we only get the savings for a half year in this calculation. I won't go into as much detail as we did before, but you can work out the numbers for yourself if you want.

First, because the price is lower, yearly cost to buy is $13,000 (520 × $25.00 each), the ordering cost works out to only $8 because we buy a half-year's supply twice during the year. Holding cost is up to $812.50, and the total effective yearly stock cost adds up to $13,820.50.

This is less than the new total yearly cost after the new price becomes effective by $648.64 ($14,469.14 – $13,820.50). But since we've only bought a half-year's supply (260 packages ordered ÷ 520 sold or used each year), our actual savings are half this figure, or $324.32. Since we earned (or saved) $324.32 for a half-year's extra stock investment of $2,925, our return on investment for this example is about 22%.

If we calculated savings for five or ten different buy-ahead quantities just as we did here, we'd find the savings increases as the buy-ahead quantity increases, up to a maximum amount. And after that, savings drops off as stock holding cost goes up faster than savings obtained from buying at the lower price. As an example, using our previous figures, if you bought ahead a supply of 400 packages, the

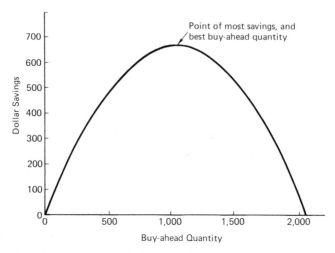

Figure 7-3. Optimum economic buy-ahead quantity provides maximum dollar savings at an optimum purchase quantity. This quantity differs from the normal economic order quantity due to the special condition of a known forthcoming price increase.

total yearly cost is $14,255.20, and your savings from buying at the new price drops to only $214.18.

If you plot on graph paper savings on the vertical axis and buy-ahead quantity, in this example, at 235 packages. This savings curve is illustrated in Figure 7-3. You *could* use this trial and error procedure to find the buy-ahead quantity that produces maximum dollar savings. But that's a lot of work and fortunately you don't have to do it. The procedure I showed earlier lets you find the buy-ahead quantity for savings directly without the need to do trial-and-error calculations. Therefore, this is an easier way of finding the economic buy-ahead quantity.

INCREASING HOLDING COST RATE TO COMPENSATE FOR ADDITIONAL RISK OF STOCKING AHEAD

Just as mentioned in chapter 6, stocking ahead greater than normal quantities involves some extra risk (as sales or use may drop from anticipated levels, or less-costly substitute products become available, or even technically superior but functionally equivalent items are introduced, obsoleting the stocked items). Also, it's possible that temporary additional storage may be required for the larger quantities of stock ordered ahead before a price increase, which is otherwise not included as a cost factor in holding cost rate normally used.

To offset this risk, it is even more logical to increase the component of holding cost allocated for required return on invested capital to a higher "risk rate." How high you set the risk rate on capital is necessarily a matter of judgment because it reflects the degree of risk you are exposed to, something only you can gauge for yourself under the immediate circumstances. If your return on capital invested is initially 15%, you may decide the required risk rate on capital is 20% or even 30% or perhaps even more. When you add this to your other holding cost components, your "at-extra-risk" holding cost rate for the economic buy-ahead quantity could be in the range of 30 to 50 percent. When at-extra-risk holding cost rates are used in the foregoing economic buy-ahead quantity formula, the effect is to reduce the buy-ahead quantity and increase the rate of return on extra capital invested in stock.

COMPUTATION BY PROGRAMMABLE CALCULATOR

You can also use a programmable pocket calculator, which further simplifies the entire procedure. I've used a programmable pocket calculator to perform this calculation automatically, (Figure 7-4). After the calculator is programmed, it's only necessary for you to punch in the applicable numbers and press the start button. The calculator takes over and works out the formula, obtaining and printing the economic buy-ahead quantity. The procedure not only finds the economic buy-ahead quantity quickly, simply, and automatically, but it also calculates the savings for any other quantity you give it should you want to know the savings at other buy-ahead quantities. Figure 7-5 is a printed tape illustrating results from the programmable calculator shown in Figure 7-4.

SUGGESTIONS FOR PRACTICAL USE

Seasonal Sales or Use. This method assumes sales or use are more or less steady. If you have a seasonal product, use the calculated buy-ahead quantity if the amount *is less than your expected* seasonal sales. If expected seasonal sales are less than the calculated buy-

Figure 7-4. A programmable calculator like that shown here can automatically perform the economic buy-ahead quantity computation.

ahead quantity, buy only the quantity you'll sell or use during the season. (The *exact* answer when you have seasonal sales is a more complex problem. If you have expensive products, get technical assistance from an industrial engineer or other consultant familiar with solving problems like these.)

Probable Price Increases. This method is designed for use when the price increase is certain—either your supplier has announced it in

520.	D⁄YR	Demand (use) per year
25.00	OLDP	Old price
27.50	NEWP	New price
235.	EBAQ	Economic buy-ahead quantity (calculated)

Figure 7-5. An illustration of the printout of the programmable calculation for economic buy-ahead quantity. First three lines are information required for the calculation, and last line is calculated economic buy-ahead quantity.

advance or you find out from a reliable source. Many companies don't announce increases in advance but just raise prices effective on announcement. If you're only 50% sure, for example, that the price increase will happen, this technique doesn't directly apply. Use this method with certain knowledge, or reasonably certain knowledge of a coming price increase.

Perishable or Dated Stock. This procedure assumes the stock you have has an indefinite shelf life. If it doesn't, don't buy more stock than you can move before the shelf life expires.

Deduct Large On-Hand Quantities. The economic buy-ahead formula assumes your on-hand quantity of an item is negligible in relation to the quantity ordered, as it was in our example (order 235 packages with 26 packages or less on hand).

If 26 packages would be actually on hand at the time the order for 235 packages were received, you could deduct the expected on-hand quantity from the economic buy-ahead quantity if significant. In this example, the economic buy-ahead quantity would be exactly 209 (235 – 26). As a practical matter, it is only necessary to do this if the on-hand quantity is large in relation to the economic buy-ahead quantity.

Order Quantity Differences. In the previous example, we've assumed that you've used the economic order quantity (EOQ) procedure for finding the quantity to order at the old and new price. If you don't use the economic order quantity method, simply substitute the order quantities you would ordinarily buy. For example, in our previous example, let's assume that items are shipped only in standard quantities of 24 packages, or some other standard unit. In both instances (the old and new price conditions), you would still order 24 packages each time. In this condition, simply substitute what you would normally order.

Buying Less Than the Calculated Buy-Ahead Quantity. If you can't buy the calculated buy-ahead quantity because of limited money or other crucial reasons, then buy as much as you can up to the economic buy-ahead quantity. Your return on investment is advantageously high even if you don't buy the indicated amount. Your rate of return on dollars invested is even higher.

If you have numerous stock items, each with price increases within a short time of each other, you may find the indicated economic buy-ahead quantity requires a total stock investment greater than the amount of money you can make available. In this instance you can increase return on the capital component of your holding cost to an arbitrarily high return on capital investment in stock, say to 35%, as an example. This in turn increases your holding cost rate even higher (say 42%, for example). This procedure assures a uniform rate of return on capital invested to stock ahead (rather than some economic buy-ahead quantities returning less and others returning more), which results if an economic buy-ahead quantity below the indicated ideal is *arbitrarily* picked.

Never buy over the economic buy-ahead quantity; savings drop off at purchase quantities in excess of the calculated buy-ahead quantity.

LIMITED-TIME BUYING DEALS

If you are offered a stock item at a temporarily reduced price (a deal with a limited-time discount—the cost goes up at the expiration of the offer), this is the same condition as a known forthcoming price increase, as we've just discussed.

Figure 7-6 illustrates this price change phenomena. The horizontal line illustrates price movement between the beginning regular price (A), the temporary period of the limited-time reduced price (C), and the restoration of the price to the original level (D).

You can see the change from price level C to price level D is the same condition as a regular price increase, as we've previously discussed. Use the same buy-ahead analysis with the special lower price as the original price of the item, and the regular (or higher price) as the new price.

Here's an example: A product you stock now costing $25 per package is offered to you for a two-week limited time at a 10% discount. The price is then $22.50 per package ($25 - 0.1 × $25). All of the previous factors are the same (you sell or use 520 each year; holding cost rate equals 25%, ordering cost is $4). However, you elect to use the holding cost rate of 30% to compensate for the

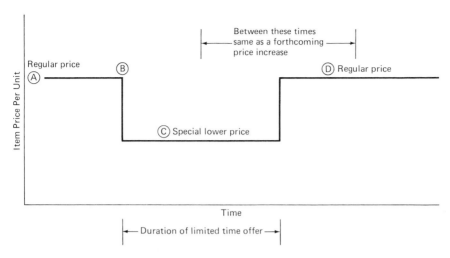

Figure 7-6. Illustration of a limited time price reduction as a comparable condition to a known forthcoming price increase.

extra business risk of buying ahead in this instance. The calculations for this limited-time deal are shown in Figure 7-7.

Limitation or Use of Procedure for Temporary Price Reductions. When you are offered a temporary price reduction as described above, use of this method assumes the price won't again be reduced before you've used or sold the quantity you've bought ahead. If it will, buy only the quantity ahead you will use before the next time the item is available at the lower price.

ECONOMIC BUY-AHEAD QUANTITY FOR PRICE INCREASES ON A QUANTITY DISCOUNT PRICE SCHEDULE

Thus far we've looked at price increases for single price products. We'll now look at a procedure for finding the economic buy-ahead quantity for a product sold under a quantity discount price schedule when a price increase is announced.

Let's go back to our original quantity discount example shown in Table 6-1 and Figure 6-1. We'll say your supplier announces a price increase of 10% effective March 1, applicable to each price bracket.

FIND TERM 1	EXAMPLE:
Step 1: Take the difference between the high and low costs (25.00 – 22.50) and multiply the difference by annual sales (520).	(25.00 – 22.50) × 520 = 1,300
Step 2: Multiply the low cost (22.50) by your holding costs rate (0.30).	22.50 × 0.30 = 6.75
Step 3: Divide the result from (1) by the result from (2) to get the answer (192.6) for Term 1.	1300 ÷ 6.76 = 192.6 (Answer, Term 1)

FIND TERM 2	EXAMPLE:
Step 4: Multiply annual sales (520) by order cost $4.00.	520 × 4 = 2080
Step 5: Multiply low cost ($22.50 by inventory holding cost rate (0.30), and by the new economic order quantity (25).	22.50 × 0.30 × 25 = 168.75
Step 6: Divide the result from (4) by the result from (5) to obtain the answer for Term 2.	2080 ÷ 168.75 = 12.3 (Answer, Term 2)

FIND TERM 3	EXAMPLE:
Step 7: Multiply the new order quantity (25) by the high cost (25.00).	25 × 25.00 = 625
Step 8: Multiply the number 2 by the low cost (22.50).	2 × 22.50 = 45
Step 9: Divide the result from (7), by the result from (8) and get the answer for Term 3.	625 ÷ 45 = 13.9

GET THE BUY-AHEAD QUANTITY:	EXAMPLE:
Step 10: Add the answers for each term and get the economic buy-ahead quantity:	Term 1 + Term 2 + Term 3 192.6 + 12.3 + 13.9 = 218.8 rounded to 219 packages

Figure 7-7. Example of calculating economic buy-ahead quantity for a limited time price reduction.

**Table 7-1. Example of Quantity Discount Price Schedule with 10%
Across-the-board Price Increase.**

PRICE BREAK REFERENCE -1-	QUANTITY FROM -2-	TO -3-	OLD PRICE[1] (BEFORE MARCH 1) -4-	NEW PRICE[2] (AFTER MARCH 1) -5-
A	1	24	$25.00	$27.50
B	25	49	23.00	25.30
C	50	99	22.50	24.75
D	100	199	21.50	23.65
E	200	299	21.25	23.38

Note 1. Same price as shown in Table 6-1.
Note 2. 10% more than old price.

The price increase is illustrated in Table 7-1, showing your old and new prices.

To determine which of these price brackets to buy in when you know of a forthcoming price increase, follow the steps below:

Step 1: Find the least-costly order quantity for the old quantity discount price schedule (as you would normally do with the price schedule in effect before March 1).

Step 2: Find the least costly order quantity for the new quantity discount price schedule that will be in effect after March 1 (although the new price will always be different, you may find yourself still purchasing in the same quantity bracket).

Step 3: Use the old price as found in Step 1 and use the new price as found in Step 2. Select an appropriate holding cost rate.

Step 4: Solve the economic buy-ahead quantity formula with the old and new prices noted in Step 3 above and the selected holding cost rate. As with the old order quantity, use the quantity you would order under the quantity discount schedule from Step 1.

Step 5: If the indicated buy-ahead quantity resulting from Step 4 is in a higher bracket with a lower price than the price originally used in Step 4 as the new price, repeat Step 4 using the lower price in the higher quantity bracket as the new price.

8. Introduction to the Line-Buy Decision: Buying a Line of Related Items On a Single Order

The regular economic order quantity is based on the ability to enter an order for any single item you stock whenever the supply gets down to a reorder point you've decided upon. This is a preferred method of ordering stock to minimize total stock costs.

However, there may be occasions when you want to order a group of related items all at one (typically from one supplier's *line* of products), even though some of the items haven't yet been sold or used down to the level of your normal reorder point. When you buy a series of stock items at the same time from one supplier's line of products, this is a *line-buy*. A line-buy differs from the normal economic order quantity and reorder point method we've previously discussed, because you order some items before your stock level is down to your regular reorder point. Because of this, for a period of time you will be overstocked relative to the quantity that you would normally buy.

When would you intentionally order early and overstock like this? We know if you order before the existing supply of a stock item is down to the correct reorder point, it increases your average inventory and in turn increases your inventory holding costs. Therefore, if the line-buy increases holding costs, why would you want to do it? The only time you would want to line buy is if there was an offsetting benefit that reduces costs more than your holding costs go up as a result of buying before your stock levels get down to the normal reorder point. Now we can ask ourselves what benefits (or requirements) justify a line buy? Here are several:

1. A supplier offers you a discount from the normal price for a specified size of a total order (such as a $1,000 order), and one item doesn't justfy an order of this size.
2. A supplier offers you a discount for a shipment of a specified size, like a carload lot.
3. The supplier offers you another tangible benefit for buying a specified minimum order or shipping load, such as paying the shipping costs you would otherwise pay for an order below the stipulated minimum size.
4. If the supplier will not ship below a specified minimum amount or shipping load, and one item of stock that you would otherwise order doesn't come up to this minimum, you must buy other items to fill the supplier's minimum. This then is a line-buy. For example, a supplier stipulates that you must have a minimum order of $1,000, or alternately will ship in truckload or carload lots only. This is not a benefit in the sense of a savings as an incentive to line-buy, but rather is a supplier's minimum limit you must accommodate because of their shipping terms.
5. You obtain an intangible benefit by purchasing a minimum order (such as early shipment of the order, expedited handling, or other items of goodwill).
6. You obtain an intangible benefit in the form of convenience through buying a supplier's line at one time. For example, the supplier's salesman is in your office or store, and it is more convenient for you to purchase all of the supply items at one time rather than ordering them individually later. In this case you would estimate the value of the intangible convenience benefit.

As an illustration, let's take the first benefit listed and discuss it further. Your supplier offers you a line-buy deal resulting in a tangible benefit -- say a 10% discount, if you buy a minimum amount ($1,000, for example) of any of the items in the entire line. In this example, the benefit is $100 (0.10 X $1,000). You may buy each individual item in any quantity you wish, but the total order must come to a minimum catolog price of $1,000. To get the line-buy benefit, you will have to buy more than your normal quantities of the items comprising the total order, and consequently you will over-stock some or possibly all of the items you buy to reach the $1,000 minimum amount. (You will also get a small secondary benefit when you overorder, because your extra ordering cost will go down since you will order in larger quantities and therefore less frequently.

The disadvantage you incur is the increased holding cost caused by overstocking some items. The decision you must make is whether the line-buy benefit ($100 in this example) offsets the increased holding cost or not. Here's the basic rule to follow: If you estimate the line-buy benefit ($100) you receive is greater than additional holding costs you incur, you go along with the line-buy. If the bene-fit is less than the additional holding costs, buy your normal quan-tity, ignoring the line-buy benefit offer.

Subjective Approach to Estimating Additional Holding Cost. If you do buy the line of merchandise costing $1,000, you actually pay $900 (1,000 – $100 discount), so in this example you have a $100 poten-tial benefit. To get this benefit you must overstock some items. The questions to answer are:

1. How much must you overstock?
2. How much will overstocking cost you?
3. Will the total cost of overstocking be more or less than the value of the benefit.

These aren't simple questions to answer, and in the final analysis your best bet is often to understand what's involved in a line-buy deal, know the value of the benefit, and make a *subjective judgment* about the amount of the extra holding cost.

Calculating Exact Additional Holding Costs. The other approach to line-buy decisions involves a quantatative analysis of the extra holding costs involved. In this approach you select items in the line that entail the least additional holding cost, and then compare exact total additional holding costs against the benefit you will receive. The problem involved is the amount of calculation required to find the optimal answer, usually requiring either a programmable calculator or other computer.

To illustrate the calculator problem, let's assume there is $600 worth of stock you'd order anyhow, leaving $400 of stock you really aren't ready to order. Your overstock isn't $400. Rather, for each stock item you order for which the on-hand quantity is more than the reorder point, it's the *difference* between on-hand quantity and your normal reorder point. This difference is the same as extra safety stock (safety stock you would not normally add). Nevertheless, you must hold this extra stock until it's sold off in the next order cycle, and pay the extra holding cost resulting from being overstocked.

Let's take a specific example for an item we'll call Product X. Your on-hand quantity is 23 units and your reorder point is 10. If you order 25 more units on a line-buy deal, your overstock will be the 23 units of on-hand stock minus the 10 units of your normal reorder point. This is 13 units in this example (23 − 10). In effect, this quantity is additional safety stock you would not ordinarily have added, but do add as a result of the early buy to take advantage of the line-buy deal. You will be overstocked these 13 units of Product X until you sell the overstock down to the original on-hand quantity of 23, putting you back into the original stock position. Selling at a rate of 10 units each month means you will be overstocked 13 units for 2.5 months (25 more units ordered divided by 10 units sold each month), equivalent to 2.5/12 of a year. Using these figures, this overstock will cost you $2.37 ($3.50 unit cost × 13 units overstocked × 2.5/12 of a year × 0.25 holding cost rate).

From this example you can see the *general formula* for the extra holding cost resulting from the line-buy for this one item is:

$$\text{Extra Holding Cost} = \begin{pmatrix} \text{Units} \\ \text{Overstocked} \end{pmatrix} \times \begin{pmatrix} \text{Fraction of} \\ \text{Year Overstocked} \end{pmatrix}$$
$$\times \begin{pmatrix} \text{Unit} \\ \text{Cost} \end{pmatrix} \times \begin{pmatrix} \text{Holding} \\ \text{Cost Rate} \end{pmatrix}$$

Substituting the specific terms we'll actually use in figuring extra holding costs, we have:

$$\text{Extra Holding Cost} = \begin{pmatrix} \text{On Hand} & \text{Normal} \\ \text{Qty at} & - \text{Reorder} \\ \text{Reorder} & \text{Point} \end{pmatrix} \times \begin{pmatrix} \dfrac{\text{Qty Ordered Early}}{\text{Sales or Use Each}} \\ \text{Month} \times 12 \end{pmatrix}$$

$$\times \begin{pmatrix} \text{Unit} \\ \text{Cost} \end{pmatrix} \times \begin{pmatrix} \text{Holding} \\ \text{Cost} \\ \text{Rate} \end{pmatrix}$$

Now substituting our example figures from above, we obtain:

$$\text{Extra Holding Cost} = (23 - 10) \times \left(\frac{25}{10 \times 12} \right) \times (3.50) \times (0.25)$$

$$\text{Extra Holding Cost} = (13) \times (0.2083) \times (3.5) \times (0.25)$$

$$\text{Extra Holding Cost} = \$2.37$$

To get a precise answer to the total cost of overstocking a selection of items to be ordered early, calculate the overstock cost for each item you order in a line-buy that you would not ordinarily yet order (were there not a line-buy benefit to offset the extra cost). You can see this calculation will require considerable work if there are numerour items in the order, a variety of items to select from, and/or there are numerous line-buy deals.

If the items involved in a potential line-buy are expensive, and/or the value of the total order is large, you will want to calculate the total extra holding cost and the difference between this extra cost and the benefit offered. If you do a line-buy like this, make your order list of otherwise unwanted stock items from those items whose on-hand quantities exceed the reorder point by the smallest percentage. Then follow the summary procedure shown below. In this way you will minimize your overstock cost and obtain a greater part of whatever benefit is offered by linebuying.

While it is relatively easy to do these calculations with a computer or programmable calculator—or even to calculate a few items by hand—in practice you will probably make a judgmental decision for low-cost items and relatively low-value orders. Your decision, however, will be better by recognizing what a line-buy is, the extra costs resulting from a line-buy, and knowing or estimating the amount of the benefit potentially offsetting the extra holding costs.

Two Alternatives for Judgmental Line-Buy Decisions.   If you adopt the judgmental decision approach to line-buy item selection, there are two alternative methods to consider:

1. Make the item selection decision each time you consider a line-buy;
2. Establish line-buy guides, often called *line points* (in the same fashion as reorder points are established), to help others to whom you may delegate a judgmental line-buy decision.

Bear in mind each of these methods is an expedient and informed estimate of the relative merits of whether or not to line buy. Let's talk about each alternative.

Each-time judgmental line-buy decision.   If you do line buy like this, make your order list of (otherwise unwanted) stock items whose on-hand quantity exceed the reorder point by the smallest percentage. Then follow the summary procedure shown below. In this way you will tend to minimize your overstock cost and obtain a greater part of the benefit offered by line buying.

SUMMARY OF THE JUDGEMENTAL DECISION FOR THE LINE-BUY PROCEDURE

STEP 1: Establish basis of line-buy minimum.   For example, you may have a line-buy minimum of a carload lot, or a specified dollar volume.

STEP 2: Determine the amount of the benefit resulting from the line-buy.   The benefit resulting may be a reduction in shipping cost, a price discount, the equivalent value of free merchandise, or possibly intangible cost resulting from convenience in ordering. Also see chapter 9 in estimating benefits.

STEP 3: Select items to line buy, causing minimum extra holding cost.   Estimate (instead of calculate) the extra holding cost to line buy the minimum quantity or dollar amounts stated. Select items whose on-hand quantity exceeds the reorder point by the smallest percentage. Estimate the approximate extra holding costs incurred, or decide if the benefit value is greater than extra holding costs.

STEP 4: Decide whether to line buy. Compare the estimated extra holding cost to line buy (Step 3) against the amount of the benefit estimated or determined from Step 2. If the line buy benefit exceeds the line-buy cost, you may be justified in the line-buy. If the line-buy cost exceeds the benefit, you may not be justified in line buying.

The essence of this decision is a comparison of the extra holding cost to you resulting from the line buy, versus the value of the benefit from the line-buy.

Establishing Line Points. Another alternative method of making the judgmental decision (instead of exact calculation of holding costs and each-time judgmental decisions) is establishing line-buy guides, called *line points.* Line points are stock quantities that enable others to make judgmental line-buy decisions by comparing on-hand stock quantity against the previously established line points to decide if the item can be included in a line-buy. If the on-hand quantity is at or below the line point, it can be included; if not, it cannot be included. All methods of establishing line points for judgmental line buying are hypothetical approximations for convenience, and are never a substitute for the exact calculation of extra holding costs—that is, they are empirical line buying guides. One approach to establishing empirical line points is simply to set a multiple of the reorder point you establish—for example, 120% of an item's reorder point. The multiple is adjusted up or down from time to time, to control how many line-buys occur. Through this line-buy point, you can delegate the line-buy decision to others with a simple (but approximate) decision-making criterion.

AVOID LINE BUYING UNINTENTIONALLY

Just as you will make a conscious decision to line-buy based on an estimate or calculated value of costs versus benefits, you will also want to be alert to not make line-buys unintentionally, when there is no benefit involved.

An unintentional line-buy could occur when a salesperson calls on you, perhaps checks your shelves for you, and assists you in writing up an order for everything you are "low on" and "need to reorder."

If you follow this procedure, you have made a line-buy, perhaps un-intentionally. To do so intentionally, you must decide if the ex-cess holding cost you'll likely pay as a result of this form of line buy-ing is less than the benefits resulting from (1) having someone else check your shelves, rather than you doing it, (2) assisting you in writ-ing the order, and (3) amortizing the cost of ordering a number of items at once.

You must also be aware that the problem may be compounded if the salesperson also determines the quantity you reorder, rather than your selecting your own economic order quantity. It is likely the order quantity suggested by a salesperson will be higher than you would normally calculate and order yourself.

In this compound event of unintentional line buying plus supplier-determined order quantities, your inventory costs will be further in-creased by an abnormally high economic order quantity plus the excess inventory carried by ordering earlier than otherwise necessary. If there is no benefit from line buying, order items individually as they reach reorder points, and at the economic order quantity you determine is best for your operations. Recognize and avoid uninten-tional line-buys without adequate offsetting benefits.

THE CONSTANT ORDER CYCLE BUYING SYSTEM AS A FORM OF LINE-BUY

We just saw it is sometimes desirable to order all items of a manufac-turer's line at one time. For some companies, the entire stock of goods is treated as one line, so to speak, and the stock room is check-ed periodically, one a week, for example, to find items which are considered "low." Items with low on-hand quantities are reordered each Monday morning or on the first and fifteenth of each month as examples.

When the entire stock is considered one line and the stock levels are checked periodically and, correspondingly, orders are entered periodically (weekly, for example), then this method is a *constant order cycle* system.

An advantage to a constant order cycle system is that on-hand stock records are not always kept. Visual inspection is made at one time, and the reordering of additional stock is scheduled for one specific day, or for specific times during a month.

The disadvantage to the constant order cycle system is that stock costs are not minimized because reorder points (if set at all) must be disregarded for some items. This means some items will be ordered before the ideal reorder point, and perhaps some items afterward. Additionally, while it is possible to establish economic order quantities for use with a constant order cycle system, in many actual systems arbitrary quantities for "minimum" and "maximum" are set. Properly used, economic order quantities are calculated as described before, and the items are ordered in economic quantities.

Recognize that the constant order cycle buying system is not as economical as the normal reorder point triggered buying system because you will buy items above and below your ideal reorder point. The constant order cycle system is a variation of the line-buy. Nevertheless, this system is used in many firms where stockouts are not critical, and the convenience of ordering at a constant time each week or month (the line-buy benefit of constant order cycle systems) outweighs the cost of keeping stock records and other extra stock costs.

9. Suppliers' Other Deals and the Concept of Landed Cost

Suppliers often offer you price incentives (or *deals*) to buy more than normal stock, or incentives to buy from one supplier rather than a competitor, and sometimes to pay earlier.

In two previous chapters we looked at two common types of suppliers' special deals. In chapter 6 we discussed how to pick the best quantity discount bracket—a quantity discount deal. Also, in chapter 7 we looked at a method of establishing purchase quantity based on a limited-time price reduction deal.

These two deals are common because they both involve known price changes as a part of the deal. In this chapter we will look at several other types of deals, plus we'll describe how to convert benefits (other than price changes) to a form convenient for analysis, and how to select the best deal that enables you to reduce stock costs.

THE CONCEPT OF LANDED COST

The actual cost of items you buy isn't necessarily the quoted or catalog price. Rather it's the total cost to you when merchandise lands in your stockroom (and therefore here called *landed cost*). Landed cost is the base cost of merchandise plus any extras you pay (like freight) minus the equivalent dollar value of any benefits you receive (like extended payment terms).

For example, if you buy 43 packages of a stock item at a catalog price of $25 per package (or $1,075 total), and freight is $200, your landed cost is $1,275 ($1,075 + $200). At this point the real cost to you is $29.65 per package, not $25 ($1,275 ÷ 43 packages). There-fore, landed cost is $29.65 per package.

In addition, if the supplier offers you a benefit—say a 5% discount off the catalog price, or $53.75 ($1,075 × 0.05)—then the value of that benefit is deducted from the cost of finding net landed cost. In this example, net landed cost is $1,221.25 ($1,075 − $53.75 + $200 freight), and net unit landed cost is $28.40 per package ($1,221.25 ÷ 43 packages). This is the unit cost to use in the economic order quantity formulas for maximum accuracy.

The point is that we will convert any deal offered to an equivalent landed cost as the first step in determining if the deal is a good one. The difference between your normal total cost (say $1,275) and total landed cost ($1,221.25) is the value of the deal benefit (in this example it's $53.75). Your supplier will want you to do something different (buy more, pay sooner, forget a competitor, etc.) in ex-change for a deal benefit. You must first find your landed cost to see whether the net benefit is worth buying more, paying sooner, or whatever.

Finding the Value of Suppliers' Promotional Benefits for Figuring Landed Cost. Suppliers frequently use freight payment as a benefit. Figuring the dollar value of freight is easy because it is usually already known in terms of its dollar value. Some benefits are not directly stated in dollars, so we convert them to their dollar equivalents, even estimat-ing if we must.

Free merchandise falls into this category: "Look, if you buy 12 of these you get one free." Of course, you don't really get one *free*, you get a benefit equivalent to the dollar value of the free item.

The free item isn't necessarily the same merchandise item you bought. It could be a different product, even something for personal use rather than retail sale. The procedure is still the same. Convert the value of the free merchandise to an equivalent benefit in dollars, reduce the total price by the benefit value, and figure the true landed cost.

Another variation of the free merchandise benefit designed to get your attention is the one-cent sale method: "Buy 12 and for one cent, get another."

What if the extra free item of benefit is something you don't really want or need? The dollar value is zero, and you figure it as no real price reduction.

Finding the Value of Invoice Dating as Deal Benefits. Postdating of invoices for goods purchased means the date of payment is postponed to the date shown on the invoice. This is commonly called *invoice dating*. For example, your supplier says, "If you will buy your entire Christmas supply now (September 1), we'll postdate this $500 invoice until December 31 and you won't have to pay until then."

This example of invoice dating is a benefit in exchange for buying a larger quantity. The benefit is three months use of $500 as operating capital in your business. (I've used three months on the assumption you'd normally receive the same goods about December 1 and pay at the end of the month. Therefore, the extra use of funds is between September 1 and November 30. Always figure the time of extra use of funds in invoice dating problems.)

Given that the extra use of funds is for three months, here's how to find the equivalent dollar value of a benefit in the form of a postdated invoice. The landed cost of your order will be $500 less the value of your use of $500 for three months or 90 days. This benefit is the same as the interest in dollars on $500 if you actually borrowed the money from a bank at the prevailing interest rate. We can figure the approximate value of the money at an interest rate of 12% per year, for example, as equivalent to 1% per month (12% ÷ 12 months). For three months, the value of the money is 3% of the total, and that comes to a benefit of $15 ($500 × 0.03).

This is the equivalent value of a three-month invoice dating of a $500 invoice when the interest rate is 12%. We reduce our invoice purchase price to $485 ($500 – $15) to obtain our actual total landed cost. You can then decide if the benefit is worth holding the extra stock you must purchase.

In this example I picked round numbers for easy illustration: 12% interest and 3-month dating exactly. What do you do if the interest rate is, say, 11.5% and the time involved in 45 days? Use a ruler and the diagram shown in Figure 9-1. Convert the days of invoice dating on the left scale (labeled Days Before Payment Due) with the interest

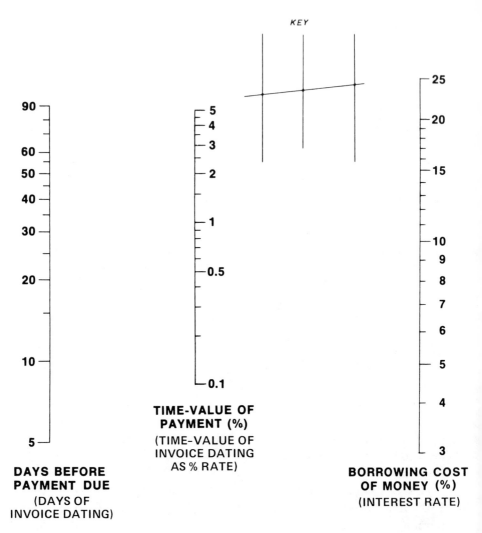

Figure 9-1. Nomogram for calculating the time-value of a post-dated invoice.

rate on the right scale (labeled Borrowing Cost of Money), and read the Time-Value of Payment in percent from the center scale. Multiply this time-value percent by the amount of the invoice to get the dollar-equivalent value of the invoicing dating. In this way you can find the equivalent dollar value for any combination of interest rates and days of invoice dating.

This may also be found by the formula:

$$\text{Time Value of Payment (\%)} = \left(\begin{array}{c} \text{Number of days} \\ \text{before payment} \\ \text{due} \end{array} \times \begin{array}{c} \text{Borrowing} \\ \text{Cost of} \\ \text{Money (\%)} \end{array} \right)$$
$$\div\ 365$$

The diagram eliminates the need to calculate this directly, and enables graphic solution to this formula by simply drawing a line. Remember to convert the result (*Time-Value of Payment %*) to a decimal rate (for example, convert 1.5% to .015). Then multiply by dated invoice amount.

Finding the Value of Chances to Win as Deal Benefits. Let's look at a benefit like a chance to win a free trip—to Bermuda, for example. Let's say the value of the trip is about $2,500. You estimate the probability of winning at about one out of a thousand (1/1000 or 0.001).

The equivalent value of a benefit involving any chance is found by multiplying the value of the trip (or benefit) ($2,500) by the estimated probability of winning (0.001). In this example, the benefit is $2.50 ($2,500 × 0.001). Although a $2,500 trip sounds like a large benefit, the real value of the benefit, $2.50, doesn't. The landed cost of a $500 order purchased to get the benefit is $497.50 ($500 – $2.50) in this example.

Finding the Value of Two or More Combined Benefits. Invoice dating and cash discount: Suppose a supplier offers you a trade discount *and* invoice dating. For example, a supplier offers a 5% trade discount and postdating permitting payment in 90 days. You have two benefits, one is the 5% trade discount off the invoice price and the other is the use of money ($500 in our previous example) for 90 days. From our previous example, we found that the time-value percent of money for 90 days (3 months) at 12% interest was 3%. Simply treat these as two separate benefits and convert them to their dollar values. Subtract the trade discount first, and figure postdating on the balance to find landed cost. Here's an example of the computation using the figures above:

Invoice Amount	$ 500.00
Trade Discount (0.05 × $500)	− 25.00
	$ 475.00
Value of invoice dating of $475 for 90 Days ($475 × 0.0296)	− 14.06
Total Landed Cost	$ 460.94

Multiple Benefits. You can find the net total benefit and therefore landed cost for any other multiple-benefit deal. Suppose a supplier offers you an apparently mind-boggling deal: a trade discount, invoice dating, free merchandise, and a chance to win a free trip. Can we unravel that? Yes, just figure the dollar equivalent of each benefit one at a time, reduce the original cost you would otherwise pay, and find the net landed cost of the order.

Here's an example: On a $500 invoice you are offered a 5% trade discount, 90 days dating, free merchandise worth $15 (to you), and a one-out-of-a-thousand chance to win an "all-expense paid" trip to Bermuda worth $2,500.

Invoice Amount	$ 500.00
Trade Discount ($500 × 0.05)	− 25.00
Sub-Total	$ 475.00
Value of Invoice Dating ($475 × 0.0296)	− 14.06
	$ 460.94
Free Merchandise	15.00
	$ 445.94
Value of Trip Chance ($2,500 × 0.001)	− 2.50
Net Total Landed Cost	$ 443.44

Picking the Best Benefit from a Series of Cash Discounts. As a promotional device, and instead of a single discount, some suppliers may offer you payment terms as optional cash-discount alternatives. For example, you may be offered a 6% cash discount if you pay in 30 days, a 4% cash discount if you pay in 60 days, or a 2% cash discount if you pay in 90 days. These are multiple-benefit options because they involve cash discounts *and* deferred payment options.

We've already discussed how you can convert a single cash discount into a dollar-equivalent value. Here, however, the problem is first finding which of the three payment alternatives is best, and after selecting one alternative for actual payment, then converting that payment alternative to its equivalent benefit in dollars.

In the first alternative you get a 6% discount off the invoice price plus the benefit of using the money in your business for 30 days. In the succeeding terms, you get progressively less cash discount but longer use of the money. Which of the three is best? First, estimate the current annual interest rate; we'll again use 12%. Then with the diagram in Figure 9-1, find the time-value of payment for each combination of days (30, 60, and 90 days, with the 12% annual interest rate). Use a ruler connecting 12% and each of the days as described previously. The time-value of money for 30, 60, and 90 days is 1%, 2%, and 3%, respectively.

Add these time-value percentages to the cash discount and you'll have the total percent value of the terms as shown in Table 9-1.

Based on an annual interest rate of 12%, the best deal is to pay in 30 days and take the 6% cash discount, because this produces the maximum total benefit. As illustrated in the last column, each of the other payment alternatives is worth progressively less in total even though you can wait to pay longer. The time-value of the money isn't worth the cut you take in the cash discount with this example. The value of the diagram in Figure 9-1 is that you can use any interest rate and days before payment, not just the conveniently even 12% annual interest and the even multiplier of 30 days we used here as an example.

Table 9-1. Example of Choosing Best Payment Terms from a Series of Discounts and Payment Dates Offered.

CASH DISCOUNT OFFERED (1)	DAYS BEFORE PAYMENT DUE (2)	TIME VALUE OF MONEY FOR DAYS IN COL. 2 (3)	TIME VALUE PLUS THE CASH DISCOUNT (COLS. 1 + 3) (4)
6%	30 days	1%	7% Best alternative
4%	60 days	2%	6%
2%	90 days	3%	5%

Finding the New Value of Multiple Trade Discounts. We've already discussed the simple discount from a list price that some supplier's offer as deal benefits. Additionally, suppliers often offer two and sometimes more successive or *chain* discounts. For example, a typical chain discount is 20% and 10%. You cannot add these two discounts directly to find total discount (30% is incorrect). This is because the first discount applies to a base price (let's say the $100 base price), and the second discount applies to the price calculated *after* the first discount. In this example the discount computation is:

Base Price	$100.00
First discount (0.20 × $100)	−20.00
Price after first discount	$ 80.00
Second discount (0.10 × $80)	−8.00
Net price after discounts	$ 72.00

You can see the total discount amount is $28 ($100 − $72), and the equivalent discount rate of the total discount is 28% (not 30%), found by dividing total discount ($28) by the base price ($100).

Instead of doing this calculation to find the benefit of a two-discount chain, you may figure the net effective discount (28%) with a formula:

$$\text{Equivalent Discount Rate} = (1\text{st rate} + 2\text{nd rate}) - (1\text{st rate} \times 2\text{nd rate})$$

With our example above we can calculate the Equivalent Discount Rate:

$$\text{Equivalent Discount Rate} = (0.20 + 0.10) - (0.20 \times 0.10)$$

$$\text{Equivalent Discount Rate} = 0.30 - 0.02$$

$$\text{Equivalent Discount Rate} = 0.28, \text{ or } 28\%$$

This rate is applied to the base price ($100) to find the benefit among ($28). For discounts with more than two discount rates in the chain, you will need to calculate each discount as originally

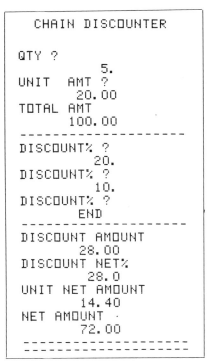

Figure 9-2. Example of automatic calculation of chain discounts. Although two discounts are shown in the chain in this example, any number of chain discounts may be found automatically.

shown rather than using the above formula to find the equivalent discount rate. As an alternative to manual calculation of three or more chain discounts, Figure 9-2 shows a printout of a chain discount calculation performed on a Texas Instruments Model TI 59 programmable calculator, programmed to figure discounts with any number of rates in the chain.

ANALYZING THE DEAL

Now that we know how to state a benefit in equivalent dollars, we can now analyze a deal to determine if it is really good. Deals are usually offered as an incentive for you to do something different. Your job is to decide if the buying action proposed is worth the benefit offered.

For many deals, just understanding the real dollar value of the benefit is enough to make a decision about whether to accept the deal or not. And once the benefit dollar value is known, the net landed cost of an item purchased may be used in the appropriate order quantity formula to find the indicated purchase quantity.

Here are several typical proposed buying actions and approaches to the buying decision:

1. Buy the single-price item from this vendor and get an offered benefit (versus not buying at all, or buying from someone else).
   Approach: Decide if the landed cost makes the merchandise more attractive than (a) buying alternate products, or (b) buying products available from alternate suppliers. If the decision is to buy, use the regular EOQ formula with the unit net landed cost.
2. Buy a larger quantity and get an offered benefit.
   Approach: Use the quantity discount analysis procedure. Use landed cost as the cost of the proposed larger quantity purchase.
3. Buy now and get a limited-time discount (or buy now before the price goes up next month, the same deal).
   Approach: Use the Economic Buy-Ahead Quantity (EBAQ) method (described in the chapter 7).
4. Buy a larger-valued order to get a discount (for example, "Buy $1,000 worth of items in the product line and get a discount").
   Approach: Use the line-buy analysis procedure (described in chapter 8).

10. Introduction to Stock-Status Accounting: Keeping Track of Sales (or Use) Rate, Quantity On Hand, and Stock Receipts

Stock-status accounting means keeping track of how much stock you have on hand, on order, and the rate at which individual stock items are used or sold. A typical handwritten stock-status accounting record is shown in Figure 10-1. There are many other options and methods available to you for obtaining stock status. This chapter will serve as an introduction to the options, enabling you to consider the system that's best for you, or even different systems for different categories of items you stock.

It's important to recognize that accounting for in-and-out transactions of your stock—that is, a stock-status accounting system—by itself isn't stock management. Rather, it provides you with *information* you need for stock management. Stock is managed (and the associated stock costs are controlled) only by the three management decisions of whether to buy, how much to buy, and when to buy. I mention this here to clarify a misconception: often handwritten or computer stock-status accounting systems are commonly called *stock-management systems*, or *inventory management systems*. In reality they are not stock-management systems without the basis for the management decisions mentioned and previously described in this book. Since most commercially available stock-status accounting

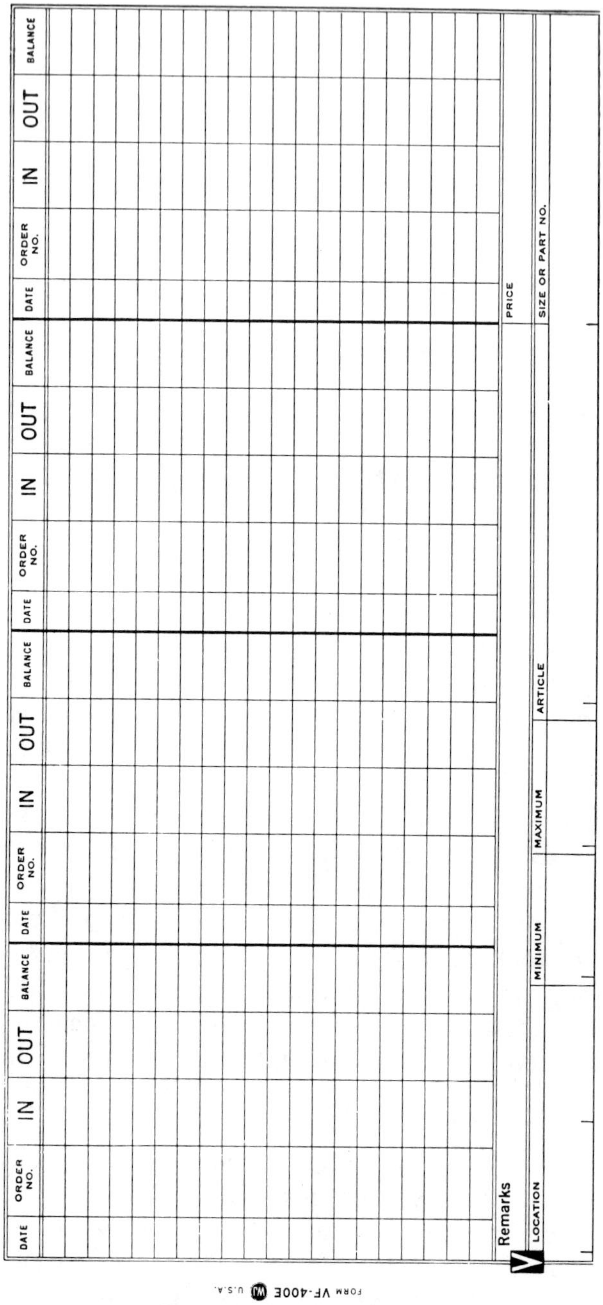

Figure 10-1. Hand-written stock status accounting record (Wilson Jones Co.)

systems do not include the decision-making component, it is inaccurate to consider them as stock-management systems. More accurately, recognize them as stock-status accounting systems.

To install a stock-status accounting system, there are three basic decisions you must make:

1. What information to keep.
2. How you will obtain the needed information.
3. What records will be kept.

WHAT INFORMATION YOU MAY ELECT TO KEEP

To make informed buying decisions, you will need to know or estimate several pieces of information about individual stock items. Let's look at each piece of information, then we'll discuss each more fully. The information you may elect to keep for each stock item is:

1. *Information About Current Stock Levels.*
   a. Quantity on hand
   b. Quantity on order
   c. Quantity back ordered
2. *Information About Stock Characteristics.*
   a. Net unit cost
   b. Sales or use rate
   c. Lead time
3. *Stock Identification.*
   a. Item name
   b. Stockkeeping unit
   c. Item stock number
   d. Storage location or bin number
4. *Current Ordering Information.*
   a. Most recently calculated economic order quantity
   b. Most recently calculated reorder point

Now let's look at important elements of this information.

1. *Quantity on hand.* It is necessary to know the quantity on hand for an item to initiate a reorder (when quantity on hand is at or below the reorder point set). A systems for signaling when the

quantity on hand is at the reorder point is always needed to initiate a timely reorder. Quantity on hand at the reorder point may be (1) calculated from in-and-out stock transactions, or (2) signaled by a two-bin system subsequently described. Quantity on hand may also be useful at other times. For instance, knowing the on-hand quantity can help you determine the amount of an item that may be committed (shipped) from on-hand stock.

2. *Quantity on order.* Quantity on order is not essential for setting normal economic order quantities or reorder points. However, it may be useful if the reorder point is greater than the economic order quantity (multiple orders outstanding), or at times when you need to know the quantity of on-hand and on-order stock that can be committed.

3. *Quantity back ordered.* If your stock system is one that permits significant back orders (see chapter 5), you may optionally record the quantity of items back ordered. If your reorder point is negative (that is, you reorder only at a prescribed quantity of back orders as explained in chapter 5), you must record quantity backordered.

4. *Net unit cost.* Net unit cost includes any price reductions or other benefits resulting from quantity purchases or other deals. Unit cost is always needed for finding economic order quantity. Unit cost is distinguished from "catalog price" or "list price." Unit cost is price less any discounts like trade or dealer discounts, plus any added costs like freight. Because the applicable cost is net cost when stock *lands* in your stockroom, it is often called *landed cost.*

5. *Item sales per unit time* (sales or use rate). Examples of sales rate are sales per week, month, or year, possibly including seasonal variations. Sales rate is either recorded or estimated, depending on the accuracy desired in calculating both economic order quantity and reorder point.

It is not possible to set economic order quantities and reorder points without reasonable knowledge of sales rate. Thus, for a person to manage inventory, it is necessary to have some information about sales rate. Conversely, recognize it is not possible to effectively manage inventory without a knowledge of item sales or use rate.

6. *Lead time for restocking.* Lead time is used with item sales rate to find cycle stock, a component of the reorder point. Often lead time is an estimate of the supplier's delivery time plus your average internal lag time for detecting low stock and then sending a replenishment order.

Once determined for a supplier, lead time for restocking is often applicable for all items the same supplier ships. Correspondingly, once average internal lag time for detecting low stock and sending a replenishment order is found for your business or institution, this internal lag time is applicable to all items you stock.

In addition to this information about stock levels and stock characteristics, you of course will need to know the cost characteristics of your business or institution for ordering and holding stock, all as previously described in chapter 3. Because ordering and holding costs change only slowly, they need to be recalculated infrequently, perhaps yearly.

INFORMATION SOURCES AND RECORDS FOR STOCKKEEPING

With the basic items of information previously listed, let's look both at sources of this information and records on which we may keep it. First, we must recognize that all stock-status systems are not necessarily based on written records because of the cost of maintaining these records (that is, the record cost exceeds the potential cost savings from stock management). (Later we will discuss how to decide between written and unwritten records for stock control.)

We may classify information for stock-status record keeping according to whether or not it's written, and then according to how this information is stored:

1.0 Written (or computer printed) stock control records
   1.1 Manual stock-status card files
   1.2 Visible records
   1.3 Computer records
      .1 Periodic computer reports, manual key data input
      .2 Real-time stock-status information, manual key data input

      .3 Real-time stock-status information, automatic data recording

2.0 Unwritten information for stock control

WRITTEN STOCK CONTROL RECORDS

Handwritten Stock Records. A typical stock record card is shown in Figure 10-1. Available in card or page form from office supply stores, this typical record is the most basic of written stock-status account records.

To begin this sytem, an original stock balance is entered on the card as a result of an initial item shipment, or from a beginning count of on-hand stock. Afterward, receipts to stock on hand ("in") and disbursements from stock on hand ("out") are written on the record, and the on-hand balance arithmetically figured. To obtain the information on stock receipts and disbursements, source records of these transactions are required for receiving reports of shipments in, for example, and or for when invoices or other documents of items sold are issued.

In addition, you may elect to also include information on these forms showing the quantity of stock on order. Although not an absolute essential, showing quantity on order permits you to (1) know the total stock you could commit when the on-order quantity is received, and (2) verify that an order for the stipulated quantity has actually been placed. Knowing this information is not required in every stock-control system.

You can see clerical effort is required to maintain any handwritten stock record—to post in-and-out stock transactions, calculate the balance on hand, and write the ending balances on the record as well. A judgment is needed of whether the cost of maintaining stock records is worth the better stock control and potentially reduced inventory cost that will result. Clearly written stock records are justified only when stock-cost reduction is greater than the increase in administrative and clerical cost. Thus, while written records provide desirable information for stock control, a decision you will make is whether to use them at all, or whether to use them only for some items you stock.

If written records *are* to be used, preprinted handwritten stock records are the quickest and least expensive to implement, and yet do not preclude using another method, perhaps a computer stock-status accounting system at a later time.

Visible Records. Visible records are a recordkeeping system in which record cards, typically 5 × 8 inch cards, are held in a tray or tub file such that an edge of the card containing one line of important information is visible (Figures 10-2 through 10-4). In this way the stock item name is displayed along with the stock number and any other important status information on colored tags. This method of handwritten record keeping is essentially the same as that described in the previous section for preprinted stock-record cards. The same source documents are also required for posting information to visible record cards.

However, the visual display is convenient for quickly locating which stock items are on order, require expediting, or are back ordered. The same level of clerical effort is required for posting in-and-out transactions and calculating stock balances, although locating records is faster because of the design of the visible record file cabinets and cards.

Computer Records. Computer stock-status records have the advantage of reducing the clerical effort required for calculating on-hand balances of inventory. Also, because computers are fast at calculating, they may also automatically recalculate economic order quantities and reorder points as changes in current usage levels occur.

Computer systems for stock-status accounting can be classified as (1) *off-line* (or *batch*) systems, and (2) *on-line* (or *immediate access*) systems.

In *off-line* or *batch* systems, in-and-out stock transaction data in the form of receiving reports, invoices, and other documents are entered in the computer system all at once as a batch, usually by keyboard entry of the data into the computer system. Typically the master file of inventory balances is updated by the computer program and a periodic report that is typically printed weekly or monthly. The information on the printed report varies with the system design, but usually corresponds to the data on handwritten records plus other information that the computer is capable of developing (updated economic order quantities and reorder points, as well as usage forecasts, for example).

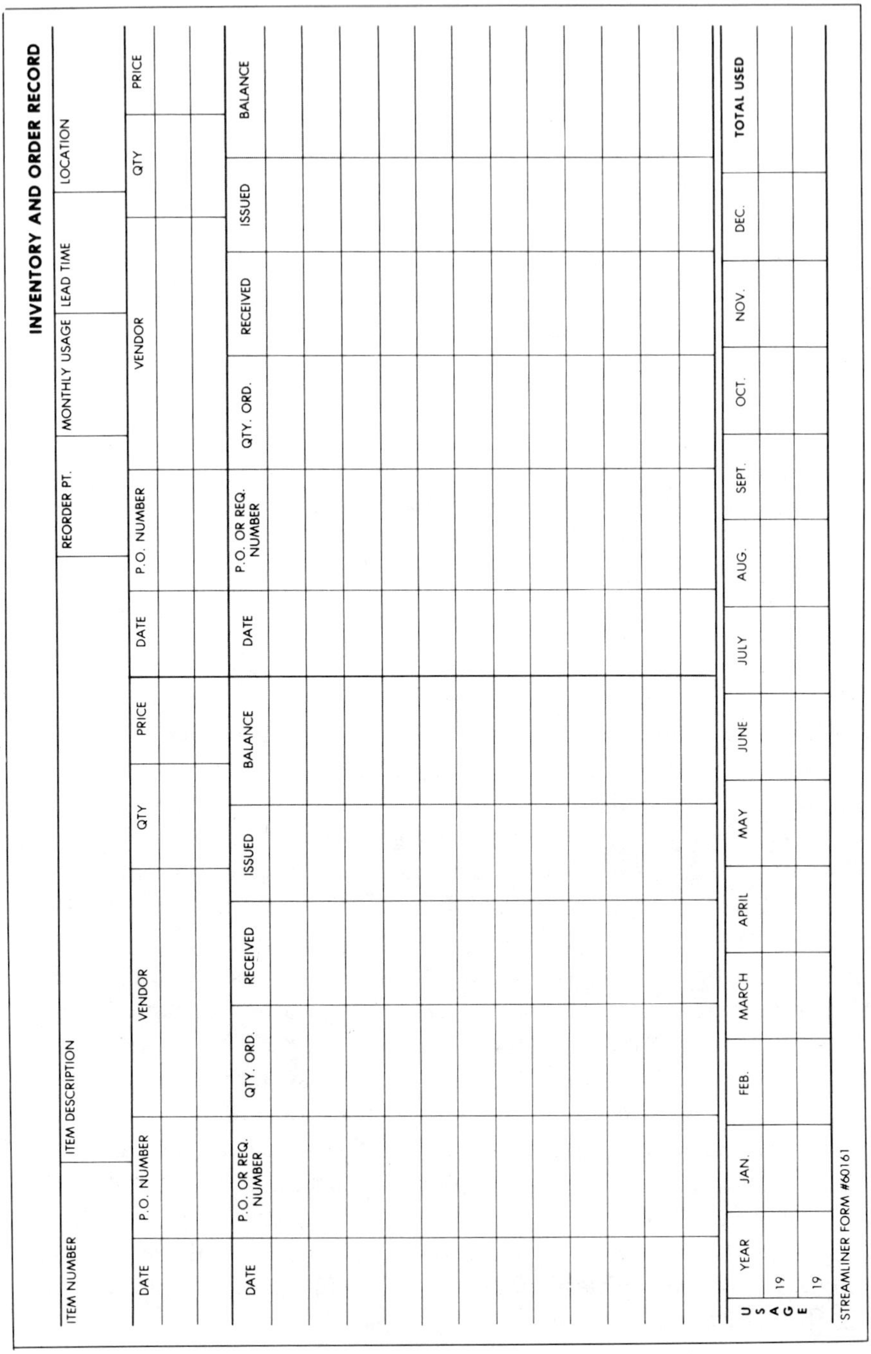

Figure 10-2. Hand-written stock status accounting record used in a card visible record system (Streamliner).

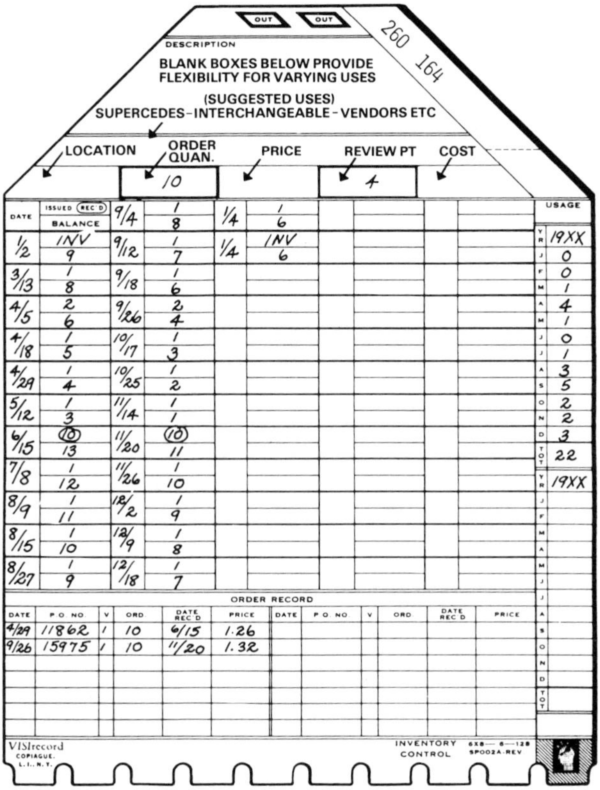

Figure 10-3. A hand written stock status accounting record used with a tub file record system (Visirecord).

Computers used this way are batch systems because all new information for a given time period that is entered in the computer updates the master file in one batch.

Batch systems are also called off-line computer systems because the user typically does not have immediate and continuing access to the master file between updating periods, and therefore is "off-the-line" with the master file between record updates.

In an *on-line* computer stock-record system, the user has immediate and continuing access to the master file, usually through a video computer terminal. Because the user is connected with the computer file continuously (that is, connected *on-line*) the stock-status file may be updated whenever convenient, even as stock transactions occur.

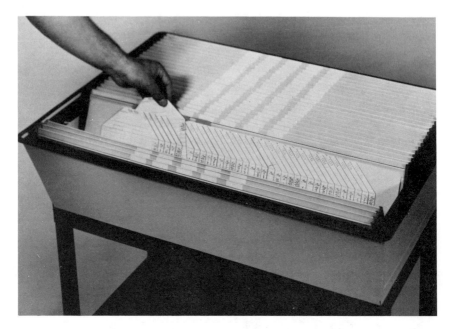

Figure 10-4. Typical tub file stock status accounting system (Visirecord).

Similarly, the stock level of any item in the master file is immediately available for display just by punching in the desired item stock number on a keyboard.

In-and-out stock transaction data may be entered into on-line computer stock records by the traditional method of computer entry, or by more advanced data-entry systems like recording bar-coded stock numbers (similar to the universal product code) with an optical wand, point-of-sale recording cash registers, or computer terminals, for example. Naturally these systems cost more than key-entry systems, and therefore must be justified by the labor savings or other advantages over keyboard data-entry systems.

The advantages of computer stock-control systems are the capability to automatically add stock receipts and subtract amounts issued, to find the new on-hand quantity (the primary stock-status accounting function) as well as the following more advanced uses:

1. Recomputing new economic order quantities and reorder points based on new sales or use experience.

2. Recalculating replenishment lead time based on the time between the date an item stock level reaches reorder point and the date of receipt of the replenishing shipment.
3. Forecasting future usage levels when a trend is established.
4. Detecting changes in usage trends.
5. Detecting and signaling when stock levels reach the reorder point.
6. Detecting and signaling when out-of-stock conditions occur as well as reporting any intermediate expediting signals before out-of-stock levels are reached.
7. Accumulation of item back orders.
8. Automatic purchase order preparation.
9. Reporting total on-hand plus on-order stock levels for separate reports of stock available for commitment.

STOCK CONTROL WITHOUT WRITTEN STOCK RECORDS

Whereas a written stock-status accounting system provides precise information about stock levels and usage, you can see that, starting with the simple card records through an on-line computer system with point-of-sale recording, the cost of these written records becomes progressively greater.

For many stock items (and for the entire stock of some firms and institutions), the cost of even simple written stock-status record systems isn't justified. In these instances it's still possible to order in economic order quantities and at predetermined reorder points without written stock-status records.

Economic order quantity calculation. Use your best estimate of item usage along with known item cost to calculate reorder points when usage reports are not available. One advantage to automatic calculation of reorder points by tables or programmable calculators is the ability to find economic order quantities for an item by bracketing high and low sales or use estimates. Often this method is adequate for establishing reasonable ballpark economic order quantities. Also consider preparing a monthly item sales or use report separately for the purpose of determining the sales rate for calculating the economic order quantities of these items.

Reorder point calculation and two-bin reorder point signaling systems. Reorder points are also easily calculated with your best estimates of sales or use, along with estimates of item lead time. The point at which stock reaches a reorder point may be signaled by a *two-bin system* (or *shelf reserve system*). The name *two-bin* results from the use of this method in industrial applications where stock items are physically stored in bins. However, it is not really necessary to use bins or other similar containers for storage at all, and for many retail and institutional applications the name *shelf reserve system* is more descriptive and apt.

For illustration, however, it's convenient to think of two separate bins or containers. The first container holds the supply of a stock item *above* the reorder point you've set. This is your normal working supply of stock. The second container holds a quantity of the stock item *equal* to the reorder point. This is your reserve supply (consisting of cycle stock plus safety stock). When it's necessary to dip into the second container of reserve stock for disbursements of the item, it is also a signal that the reorder point has been reached, and a reorder of the item is required. Often a highly visible card is kept in the second container and sent to the buyer or stock manager as notification to reorder. (Of course you will continue to use the reserve supply until a new shipment is received. When you receive your new shipment, you will then restore the reserve supply to the quantity you've set for the current reorder point.)

In this way the reorder point for the stock item is signaled without the necessity of having a written stock-status accounting record, otherwise required to indicate low stock level. This method is applicable to a wide variety of retail, institutional, wholesale, manufacturing and other commercial applications where cost and other circumstances make written records undesirable.

You can see that it is not necessary to physically use two bins. Rather, any reliable method of separating stock into a working supply and a reserve supply equal to your reorder point will signal stock levels passing through the reorder point. For items that are stacked in containers or other packages, with the containers on the top representing stock used first, this signal may be inserted in the stack where the items in the bottom of the stack comprise the reserve supply.

Any other method of distinguishing between the working supply and reserve supply of stock may be used.

HYBRID SYSTEMS FOR STOCK CONTROL

It is possible to combine some elements of written and unwritten stock control systems, including computer techniques. Figure 10-5 illustrates a computer run for stock items in which economic order quantities and reorder points are computer prepared for a range of usages above and below the previous year's usage, comprising an ordering guide for each stock item. A short table is created for each item providing stock managers with a convenient table to look up economic order quantities and reorder points for usage levels they'll likely encounter. Along with this ordering guide, a shelf reserve system is used for signaling low stock for most items. The combination represents a hybrid system of written records (the annually printed ordering guide) and the shelf reserve system, thus requiring no stock-status records.

NUMBERING SYSTEMS FOR STOCK-STATUS ACCOUNTING

In written stock-status accounting systems, it's desirable to number stock items for reference and filling convenience. This section shows you how to establish numbering systems for this purpose.

Numeric codes are usually the most convenient and efficient codes for stock numbering, particularly when computers are used (or will be used in the future). Sometimes alphabetic characters have been used as a part of item codes, frequently to help distinguish item characteristics. For example, a green item might be coded 2406-GN. Another identical item, except in purple, might be 2406-PURP. The "GN" and "PURP" are memory aids sometimes referred to as *mneumonic codes*, meaning memory-aid codes. While convenient for numbering product characteristics, they cause problems. The codes are inconsistent because 2406-GN is a six-character code and 2406-PURP is an eight-character code. Additionally, this example combines numbers and alphabetic characters, which can be more costly to file and retrieve in both manual and computer systems. Therefore we will use as examples numeric codes of consistent digit size.

INVENTORY ORDERING GUIDE

COTTON TAPE 1/2 X 007

1. PROD CODE = 21-16454	8. NO. REP CYCLES = 3.0
2. STD UNIT - RL	9. WKS LEAD TIME - 4
3. NET COST - .24	10. PROT. FACTOR - 1.85
4. ANNUAL USAGE - 1,104	11. SAFE STK COST - .82
5. COST OF SALES - $265	12. CYCLE STOCK - 85
6. AVG INV.INVEST - $45	13. SAFETY STOCK - 17
7. CURRENT EOQ - 373	

Q/MO.	Q/YEAR	EOQ	ROP
83	994	354	93
88	1054	364	98
93	1114	375	103
98	1174	385	108
103	1234	394	113
108	1295	404	118
113	1355	413	123
118	1415	422	128
123	1475	431	133
128	1535	440	138
133	1596	449	143
138	1656	457	148

COTTON TAPE 3/4 X 007

1. PROD CODE = 21-16462	8. NO. REP CYCLES = 6.9
2. STD UNIT - RL	9. WKS LEAD TIME - 4
3. NET COST - .31	10. PROT. FACTOR - 1.85
4. ANNUAL USAGE - 4,583	11. SAFE STK COST - 2.17
5. COST OF SALES - $1,421	12. CYCLE STOCK - 353
6. AVG INV.INVEST - $104	13. SAFETY STOCK - 35
7. CURRENT EOQ - 669	

Q/MO.	Q/YEAR	EOQ	ROP
344	4125	634	350
365	4375	653	370
385	4625	672	391
406	4875	690	411
427	5125	707	431
448	5375	724	451
469	5625	741	471
490	5875	757	491
510	6125	773	511
531	6375	789	531
552	6625	804	551
573	6875	819	571

COTTON TAPE 1 X 007

1. PROD CODE = 21-16470	8. NO. REP CYCLES = 6.5
2. STD UNIT - RL	9. WKS LEAD TIME - 4
3. NET COST - .36	10. PROT. FACTOR - 1.85
4. ANNUAL USAGE - 3,528	11. SAFE STK COST - 2.16
5. COST OF SALES - $1,270	12. CYCLE STOCK - 271
6. AVG INV.INVEST - $98	13. SAFETY STOCK - 30
7. CURRENT EOQ - 544	

Q/MO.	Q/YEAR	EOQ	ROP
265	3175	517	273
281	3368	532	289
297	3560	547	304
313	3752	561	320
329	3945	576	336
346	4137	590	351
361	4330	603	367
377	4522	616	382
393	4715	629	398
409	4907	642	413
425	5100	655	429
441	5292	667	444

COTTON TAPE 1 1/4 X 007

1. PROD CODE = 21-16472	8. NO. REP CYCLES = 1.3
2. STD UNIT - RL	9. WKS LEAD TIME - 4
3. NET COST - .44	10. PROT. FACTOR - 1.85
4. ANNUAL USAGE - 121	11. SAFE STK COST - .53
5. COST OF SALES - $53	12. CYCLE STOCK - 9
6. AVG INV.INVEST - $20	13. SAFETY STOCK - 6
7. CURRENT EOQ - 91	

Q/MO.	Q/YEAR	EOQ	ROP
9	109	87	14
10	116	89	14
10	122	92	15
11	129	94	16
11	135	96	16
12	142	99	17
12	149	101	18
13	155	103	18
14	162	106	19
14	168	107	20
15	175	110	20
15	182	112	21

Figure 10-5. Printout of precalculated ordering table for economic order quantity and reorder point for a series of products.

You will keep a stock record on each item you stock, even though the item differs only in package or container size, color, or other minor characteristic. Each different item on which you keep a stock record comprises a separate *stock keeping unit* (abbreviated SKU). A first step, therefore, is to make a list of separate SKUs you will have and find the total number of stockkeeping units. This information enables you to create an initial record of items in your stock-status accounting system.

Often 3 X 5 cards are convenient for this purpose. Write the item name of the stockkeeping unit as you want to refer to it and the standard unit size (each, 16-ounce package, etc.). If you wish, the stockkeeping units you establish may be grouped together—by suppliers for example. If you do this keep your 3 X 5 cards of stockkeeping units organized in these groups.

Decide on Code Size and Structure. Let's take the example of 750 stockkeeping units listed on 3 X 5 cards in alphabetic sequence by name. (In practice you may use any other logical sequence other than alphabetic should you desire to do so). For the moment, we'll assume there is no need to keep these organized by groups of suppliers or by any other characteristic. Therefore, we want to number these 750 stockkeeping units in alphabetic sequence.

Because there are 750 items, you need at least 3 digits in the code, enabling you to number 999 possible items—1 through 999. However, if only 3 digits are used there's little room for adding new items to your stock later; there is room for only 249 new stock items (999 – 750). Additionally, if you use only 3 digits, room for some of the possible new items you'll add later may not exist in the proper alphabetic slots in which you'd like to add them.

Therefore, instead let's use a 4-digit number, providing coding for numbers 1 through 9999. Now we will have adequate numbering room to proportionately space numbers used for the 750 items you have now, and adequate room later to add new stockkeeping units in the proper alphabetic position.

Determine the Numbering Skip Inverval. To keep the alphabetic spacing proportional, we'll want to number the first item with a low number and the last item with a high number. This is accomplished with a *skip interval* for numbering each item. For example, a skip interval of 10 means we would number the first item 10 (actually 0010), the second 0020, and so on. With a skip interval of 10 the last number is 7500 (750 times 10). Therefore, a skip interval of 10 will not use all of the available numbers, and those between 7500 and 9999 would be wasted.

However, we can find the skip interval that would use all the numbers by dividing the available numbers (9999) by the number of stockkeeping units to be numbered (750). In this example we obtain a skip interval of 13.3 (9999 divided by 750). Because we will use whole numbers only, we round down to a skip interval of 13. Now we'll number the first item 0013, the second 0026, and so on. The 750th stock item will be numbered 9750, effectively using most of the available 9999 numbers. A 4-digit number provides adequate room to add new stock items in this example.

Group Codes. The previous example was one for a simple serial code—serial because all items are numbered sequentially rather than in groups. We could also number stock items in groups by establishing a *group code*. A group code is one where one or more digits are used to identify groups of related stock items. Each stock item is individually numbered serially within the group code. For example, let's change the previous example to include the same 750 units, but grouped by 5 main suppliers. Additionally, you stock other items from miscellaneous suppliers. You'd like to keep your stock records separated according to main suppliers and miscellaneous suppliers, and therefore we'll establish a supplier group code with the thousands digit of the 4-digit number as follows:

> 1XXX—Main supplier 1
> 2XXX—Main supplier 2
> 3XXX—Main supplier 3
> 4XXX—Main supplier 4
> 5XXX—Main supplier 5
> 6XXX—Other miscellaneous suppliers
> 7XXX—Unused
> 8XXX—Unused
> 9XXX—Unused
> 0XXX—Unused

Within each supplier's group code, the stockkeeping units furnished by that supplier are numbered sequentially within the group. Since each supplier will likely have a different number of stockkeeping units you use, you will need to determine the skip interval for the products within each supplier's group code. You are not limited to 1-digit group code, but may also use 2, 3, or even more digits for the group code, depending on how many groups are to be coded. For convenience you may wish to separate the group code and the serial code of items within the code by a dash, as, for example, 1-XXX. For complex codes like 123-XXX, you can see the dash helps you to remember the digits or to separate them for writing convenience. Just as you could use a group code to identify different suppliers, you may use a group code to identify any other product characteristic you wish.

Once you establish these group codes, they become the primary identifying characteristic by which you will identify the product when you refer to this item on receiving reports, invoices, catalog numbers, and, of course, stockkeeping records.

11. Forecasting Item Sales or Use for Better Stock Management

Chapters 2 and 4 showed you how to make decisions about how much and when to buy. Each of the methods used for finding the most economic solution to these questions is based on an estimate of past stock sales or use. Typically, the estimate of stock sales or use is based on *past* information about item demand—obtained from your stock-status reports or sales analysis. On the other hand, item use or sales rates may simply be based on your informed judgment, or that of a manager who works for you ("I think we average about three packages each week.").

Sales or use of some items you stock will climb upward because of increasing demand. Correspondingly, demand for other stock items will trend downward, and others will have a steady level of use. However, if you use only past item sales or use data for decision-making, sales or use figures will be wrong for those items whose sales or use is trending up or down.

For stock items trending up or down, you can better manage stock and improve profits if you make buying decisions based on expected demand for stock, rather than past or historical demand. Figuring the expected demand for stock during the forthcoming week or month can mean either making an informed estimate ("For the next several weeks, I think we'll average selling about five packages a week"), or using one of the easy arithmetic tools for forecasting stock demand.

Because of the many items carried in a typical inventory, it is frequently more advantageous to use one of the arithmetic methods to provide a more accurate estimate of next period sales or use of a given item, rather than attempting to do it by judgment alone. This chapter contains several practical methods you may use for forecasting stock sales or use rate.

We look now at methods for (1) cause-and-effect forecasting, (2) trend extension, (3) moving averages, and (4) exponential smoothing.

CAUSE-AND-EFFECT FORECASTING

Cause-and-effect forecasting of future stock requirements is presented here first because whenever it's possible to accomplish, it's one of the best forecasting procedures. Cause-and-effect forecasting means you relate the specific demand for a stock item (the effect) to one or more specific reasons why the demand will occur (the cause or causes).

For example, let's say you are the principal supplier of Item X, which you sell to fifty manufacturers throughout the country who are regular customers for this item. Your sales representatives ask each customer to tell you their individual requirements for this item based on their manufacturing plans. With the total of these known requirements (the cause), you know the individual aggregate demand for Item X (the effect).

Here's another example: You stock a supply of Item Y in a hospital. Item Y is used in a new medical procedure. Because of the increasing use of the medical procedure, in turn known by the level of use by each physician for each patient (the cause), you can estimate the increasing total demand of Item Y (the effect).

On a more advanced level you may find that subsequent demand for some of your products correlate to statistical measurements like housing starts. In this event, you can correlate housing starts to your sales and thereby establish another cause-and-effect relationship.

You can see from these examples that the pattern of cause-and-effect forecasting requires that (1) you know of a specific relationship between the cause and effect ("We usually use six Y items every time we do this medical procedure), and (2) you have access to information about the incidence of the causers ("We will do two of these medical procedures on everyone admitted to the hospital).

Actually, if you know the exact relationship between cause and effect ("We *always* use six Y items . . ."), then this isn't a projection, strictly speaking, but rather a known deduced requirement.

I've mentioned this method of cause and effect first because it's often the best and most accurate method of forecasting if you can get the needed cause-and-effect information. Often it's not possible to obtain this information. Sometimes obtaining it is possible, but not practical due to the costs required.

Since cause-and-effect forecasting must be done on a one-at-a-time basis for each item, it is likely only justified for expensive stock items, those with high use rate, or items for which avoiding stockouts is critical. While these are significant disadvantages to cause-and-effect forecasting, if it is possible at all, it is also a reliable method of signaling turning points or major changes in demand for an item, often difficult to detect by other methods.

TREND PROJECTION

Trend projection means that we assume that whatever has caused an up or down trend in the past will continue to cause the same pattern of trend in the future, or at least in the near future. When the quantity sold (or used) for a previous week or other time period is plotted on graph paper, you can see the trend. Quantity is usually plotted on the vertical scale (or Y axis of the graph), and time (days, weeks, or months) on the horizontal scale (or X axis of the graph). Points plotted on an X- and Y-axis graph represent historical sales or use for each previous time period. These points are represented by a line that most closely fits all the points, and the *trend line* plotted on the graph is projected to the week or month for the upcoming forecast. (Sometimes this is also called trend-line projection.)

Whereas cause-and-effect forecasting related demand for an item to a specific cause, trend forecasting correlates item demand to days, weeks, or months of time *and requires the assumption that the-cause-and-effect that occurred previously will continue in the same way during the upcoming forecast period.*

Visual Trend Projection. The easiest-to-see trend projection method is that of actually plotting historical sales or use data on graph paper.

Although this usually isn't a practical way to do trend forecasts for many items, because of the time and effort required, we will look at the technique nevertheless because it helps us understand a method I'll show you in a moment that *is* practical.

Once you've plotted the points representing historical sales or use of a stock item, take a clear plastic ruler and lay it over the plotted points. Align the ruler so the distance from the edge of the ruler to each plotted point is as close as possible. Draw the line that makes the best fit through all the points. This is the trend line, also called a *regression line.* Extend the line to the right for the next time period. The point on the extended portion of the line at the intersection of the next time period (February) is the quantity projected by the trend line. Remember this projection requires the assumption that the causes of the sales or use in the past will continue over the forecast period in the same pattern.

In the above example we've assumed that the plotted points approximate a straight line. Often they do, particularly over short periods of time, several months perhaps. Sometimes, however, the plotted points look more like a curve. Either draw the curve free-hand, or even better, use a flexible curve available from many drawing supply stores.

Calculated Trend-Line Projection. The techniques described above illustrate how its possible to graphically forecast item sales or use trend by plotting a graph and visually projecting the trend line (or curve). Individually plotting this historical data soon becomes impractical for more than just a few items. Fortunately, there's another method of trend projection that achieves the same results without actually plotting the graph. If you studied algebra in school you may recall that a line drawn on a graph is also represented by a formula—an equation using X and Y coordinates to show where the line goes on a graph. The calculated trend projection is based on automatic calculation of the formula for the trend line of an item's sales or use (you don't have to do it).

Once the formula representing the line is known, this same formula is solved (again automatically) to find the forecast trend for next month's sales or use. All of this is the exact equivalent of actually plotting the graph and extending the trend line with a ruler, except of course we don't have to spend the time plotting. More importantly, we really don't have to know anything about algebra or the formulas representing the lines. All we need to know is how to punch a few buttons on a preprogrammed hand-held calculator like the one shown in Figure 11-1.

Several pocket calculators with preprogrammed trend-line computational capability (at the time this is written) are the Hewlett-Packard 38, and Texas Instruments MBA business calculator. Additionally, virtually all programmable calculators or pocket computers are capable of performing this forecast, including the Hewlett-Packard HP 41C, Texas Instruments' TI 58 and TI 59 calculators, and the Radio Shack TRS 80 pocket computer.

More complete instructions for calculator-generated regression lines are contained in the instruction manual for these programmable calculators and pocket computers. Although I've mentioned this calculation with a preprogrammed hand-held calculator as a simple method, obviously a larger computer is capable of the same calculated

Figure 11-1. The Texas Instruments MBA pre-programmed calculator (Texas Instruments).

trend-line projection with an appropriate program. Often simple calculation of a trend line is accurate for many stock-forecasting needs. However, we can now consider some further refinements to trend forecasting should you desire to use them in your stock-management system.

In addition to calculating a forecast, you may also obtain an index of how closely the historical data comes to the calculated line. The index that describes this correlation or lack thereof is the *coefficient of correlation*. A coefficient of correlation of 1.0 is a perfect correlation, and 0.0 is no correlation. Remember that the coefficient of correlation only indicates how well the line fits the historical data points, and *not necessarily* how accurate the forecast will likely be, because the accuracy of the forecast also depends on the assumption (we made earlier) that the same past causes of sales or use will continue in the future.

Calculated Trend-Curve Projection. Just as it is possible for plotted past sales or use data to form a line, it is also possible for past data to take the form of a curve. And just as it is possible to calculate a trend line, it is also possible to calculate a trend curve. Since several different curve choices are possible, a coefficient of correlation for each possible curve that could be used is calculated, and the one with the best fit (as indicated by the highest coefficient of correlation) is selected for the forecast. The hand-held calculator necessary to perform this more advanced calculation and analysis of best fit is one of the programmable calculators like the Texas Instruments Model 59, and the Hewlett Packard Model 41C (at the time this is written). The program description for the curve-fit program that is entered to the Texas Instrument's Model 59, for example, is available from the Texas Instrument's Professional Program Exchange (PPX), P.O. Box 53; Lubbock, TX 79408.

Just as you may calculate the trend-line projection on a larger computer, so may the trend-curve projection be similarly computed with the appropriate computer program.

Limitations of Simple Trend Projection. The principal limitation of the trend projection is that it may not clearly signal major changes in the trend—for example, from a down trend to an up trend, or from one rate of change to another. That is, the trend forecast will overproject (up or down trends) when the trend changes. There are more advanced indicators for detecting *tracking errors* that may signal a trend change. If you desire to install a more advanced forecasting system that will not only forecast future trend but also signal major changes in trend, see the book references at the end of this chapter.

A second limitation of the trend projection is that the term of projection must be relatively short—one week, one month, or possibly one quarter. The longer the forecast time, the greater the chance that the necessary assumption (of no change in past cause-and-effect relationship during the upcoming forecast period) will be invalid.

ORDINARY MOVING-AVERAGE

Another method of estimating next-period sales or use for an item, as well as removing short-term random fluctuation in the trend, is a *smoothing* method. One smoothing method is the *moving-average*. In this simple method, we take the total item demand for several previous months (say three months: January, February and March), total them, and divide by three (number of months included). This becomes the estimate for the April demand, the next month. In formula form, the April projection is:

April Estimate

$$= \frac{(\text{January actual}) + (\text{February actual}) + (\text{March actual})}{3}$$

For each month after April, the oldest month is dropped out of the moving average and unit sales or use for the most recent month is added in.

You can change the emphasis of the oldest and most recent month's sales with a moving-average forecast by changing the number of months averaged. When fewer months are averaged, more emphasis is given to recent sales or use. The greater the number of months included, the more the emphasis is on earlier sales.

As we can see, the ordinary moving-average isn't really a forecast, but rather an arithmetic average of past sales or use for the most recent months included in the moving-average. Its purpose is to reduce or dampen any wild or random fluctuation in demand around the average sales or use for the last several months. Therefore, the ordinary moving-average will effectively reduce any misleading wild fluctuations, but will also project *less* than the actual sales or use quantity of a pure uptrend, and *more* than the actual sales or use in a pure downtrend. That is, the moving-average will lag an actual trend.

The reason this lag occurs is the moving-average doesn't "know" if the trend is a pure trend or a wild fluctuation trend, and favors eliminating the wild fluctuation possibility.

WEIGHTED MOVING-AVERAGE

You may also use a weighted moving-average. The weighted moving-average can be arranged to give more emphasis to recent sales or use, and therefore lag trends less. In this smoothing option, you assign the weight each previous month's sales has on the forecast. For example, suppose you think March sales are three times more important than January sales, and February sales twice as important as January sales. Then your weighted moving-average forecast is:

$$\text{April Projection} = \frac{1 \text{ (Jan. actual)} + 2 \text{ (Feb. actual)} + 3 \text{ (Mar. actual)}}{6}$$

When using this method, you normally divide by the sum of the weights (1 + 2 + 3 = 6) instead of the sum of the number of months.

An equivalent arithmetic form of the April forecast in which each month's weighting coefficient is determined by simply dividing by six, is:

April Projection

$$= \tfrac{1}{6} \text{ (Jan. actual)} + \tfrac{2}{6} \text{ (Feb. actual)} + \tfrac{3}{6} \text{ (March actual)}$$

Or, in decimal form:

April Projection

$$= 0.167 \text{ (Jan. actual)} + 0.333 \text{ (Feb. actual)} + 0.5 \text{ (Mar. actual)}$$

You can see you may weight each month however you choose, to give more or less emphasis to past sales or use experience. For example, you could also weight the months shown above with the following weighting coefficients:

April Projection

$$= 0.2 \text{ (Jan. actual)} + 0.3 \text{ (Feb. actual)} + 0.5 \text{ (Mar. actual)}$$

The sum of the weighting coefficients you choose must equal one (in this example, 0.2 + 0.3 + 0.5 = 1).

The weighted moving-average (weighted more heavily toward most recent months as shown above) eliminates some of the insensitivity to recent sales or use trend resulting from the ordinary unweighted moving-average. It is less sensitive to concluding that every fluctuation is wild, and will be closer to a pure trend than the ordinary moving-average.

To use either the ordinary or weighted moving-average for smoothing item sales or use experience for any large number of stock items, either a programmable calculator or a computer is desirable because of the amount of calculations and data involved.

EXPONENTIAL SMOOTHING

Although moving-averages are simple to understand and easy to use for only a few items, the moving-average method becomes unwieldly as more stock items are forecasted. This is because of the need to keep monthly data on hand for the many number of months used in the moving-average. For example, if a use forecast for 100 items is made and 3 months are in the moving-average, then 300 monthly sales figures must be available for computing the moving-average. And because keeping up with all these figures plus doing the necessary calculations is a lot of work, moving-averages are often not used even though they are one of the simplest methods to understand.

Another equally good smoothing and forecasting method that reduces this data-storage problem has the five-dollar name *exponential smoothing*, but don't let the name bother you. The formula for this is easy to figure:

Forecast for next month

= 0.3 (*Actual* sales or use this month)

+ 0.7 (*Forecast* for this month made last month)

Now it's only necessary to keep the previous *forecast* for each item, and the data storage is reduced from 300 monthly sales figures (in the previous example) to only 100, plus the calculation is quicker. Item forecasts are easily made with a simple pocket calculator.

The 0.3 and 0.7 in the formula are typical weighting constants used with the exponential smoothing method. These two weighting constants allow you to adjust the sensitivity of the forecast between the most recent and previous months, similar to the way the weighted moving-average adjusts the sensitivity between the most recent months. In fact, adjusting the two weighting constants lets you come close to any combination of weighted moving-average you might choose without storing all of the previous month's data, only the forecast from the last month.

Notice that the sum of the two weighting constants is 1.0 (0.3 + 0.7 = 1.0). Therefore, once you set the first smoothing constant (0.3 in this example), you automatically know the second weighting constant because you obtain it by subtracting from the first one (1.0 − 0.3 = 0.7). Therefore, if a represents the first weighting constant ($a = 0.3$), then the second weighting constant is $1 - a$. In general form, the formula is written:

Forecast for next period

= a (Actual demand for current per period)

+ ($1 - a$) (Forecast demand for current period)

By setting a high or low, you may assign proportionately more or less weight, respectively, to the current-period actual demand (and correspondingly less or more weight to the previous period's experience).

For further information about forecasting, see: *Forecasting Methods for Management*, 2nd edition, by Wheelwright and Makridakis

(John Wiley & Sons 1977), the *Business Forecasting Methods*, by H. D. Wolfe (Holt, Rhinehart and Winston, 1966).

These books will provide you with business forecasting methods not possible to include in this chapter. For example, methods for forecasting seasonal factors that we've not discussed here are included in these references.

12. Balancing Overall Inventory Investment with Business Sales or Operating Levels

As your business grows and sales increase, you are correspondingly justified in increasing your stock investment. Adding more on-hand stock is appropriate regardless of whether sales or use increase from business growth or from seasonal factors—Christmas, for example. In either case, if you don't increase your stock levels with sales increase, your operating costs will go up because you'll have to reorder more frequently than is ideal, you'll experience more frequent stock-outs, and you'll lose profit from missed sales.

And if sales go down for any reason, your stock investment should correspondingly decrease. If you carry too much stock after sales have reduced after a Christmas selling season, for example, your cost will increase because of the extra holding cost resulting from carrying too much stock.

These same factors apply to nonbusiness institutions: As operating levels increase or decrease, stock levels must correspondingly be adjusted or costs will rise.

How much stock is too much and how much is too little is controlled for individual items you stock by the economic order quantity formula.

You will recall this formula is:

$$\text{Economic Order Quantity} = K\sqrt{\frac{\text{Yearly Item Unit Sales or Use}}{\text{Item Unit Cost}}}$$

where K is an index number typically between 3 and 9, based on your ordering and holding costs.

Remember the yearly item unit sales or use estimate in the formula? Increasing or decreasing your estimate of annualized sales for each stock item increases or decreases your order quantity, and consequently your average on-hand inventory for each stock item (since average inventory is approximately one-half the order quantity). Therefore, the EOQ formula *automatically* raises and lowers your stock investment when you raise or lower item sales or use in this formula. Therefore, if you do a correct job of estimating upcoming sales or use levels, the EOQ formula will appropriately increase or reduce your stock levels and stock investment for you.

This automatic adjustment of your inventory investment is keyed to your estimates of ordering and holding costs, which combine to form the index number K in the EOQ formula. There are reasons other than these ordering and holding cost factors for ordering more or less than the quantity normally indicated by the EOQ formula.

For example, if your business or operation is growing rapidly, and you have used all funds available for stock investment, you must (temporarily at least) limit stock investment by holding down the size of order quantity. Your operations will be slightly out of tune, so to speak, and your total ordering cost will go up because of more frequent stock orders going out and more frequent stock shipments coming in—more frequent than you would prefer if there were not limits or constraints on funds available for stock investment.

A similar condition could occur if you've completely outgrown your stockroom or warehouse and there's no other available storage space. For the time being, you must make do with the storage space you've got and hold down stock levels. In both instances you'll need to reduce on-hand stock levels, primarily by cutting order quantities, and secondarily by not stocking any marginally needed items.

In the following sections, we'll look at several indicators of appropriate stock levels, and then how to proportionately correct high or low stock levels based on these indications.

ANALYSIS OF INVENTORY LEVELS BY RATIO ANALYSIS

One method of deciding if total inventory investment is high or low is by analyzing the ratio of your overall business activity to average stock investment. In business, overall activity is usually indicated either by yearly net sales or yearly cost of sales.

In nonbusiness institutions, comparable revenues may be used instead of sales figures. For example in a hospital it could be revenue for services. It is also possible to develop and use some other activity index. For example in a hospital in lieu of revenues, the number of patient-days may be an activity index for gauging inventory levels. As another example for an aviation unit, hours flown is a possible activity index.

The business ratios typically used to analyze appropriate stock levels are the yearly cost-of-sales-to-stock-investment ratio, the yearly sales-to-stock-investment ratio, and the stock-investment-to-sales-as-a-percent ratio (reciprocal of yearly sales-to-stock-investment ratio times 100). All three are gauges for establishing appropriate total level of stock investment. Let's now look at each.

Ratio of Yearly Cost-of-Sales to Average Stock Investment. Let's assume your yearly cost-of-sales is $1,200,000, as shown on your year-end income and expense statement:

Sales	$2,000,000	100%
Cost-of-Sales	1,200,000	60%
Gross Margin	$ 800,000	40%

You've determined your average stock investment during the year is $300,000. To find this, you obtained the inventory investment from your balance sheet for each quarter (or month), totaled them, and found the average by dividing by 4 (or 12 if you did this monthly). The average investment you found to be $300,000.

Therefore, the ratio of cost-of-sales to average stock investment is:

$$\text{Ratio} = \frac{\text{Cost-of-Sales}}{\text{Average Stock Investment}} = \frac{\$1,200,000}{\$ \ 300,000} = 4$$

This ratio is also known as the inventory turnover ratio because your $300,000 worth of stock is sold, or "turned over," four times during the year. This is so because you've sold goods *costing* $1,200,000.

Inventory turnover ratio is ofted misinterpreted. An implication is that the higher the inventory turnover ratio the better your profit, and therefore use the turnover ratio as an ordering guide for individual items (which is not valid).

However, a valid use of the ratio of cost-of-sales to average inventory investment is comparing your ratio to the same ratio as others in your line of business. These *inventory turn* figures are often collected by industry associations and others, and you may use these as comparative guides for your own turnover ratio.

Also, you may note from time to time your approximate inventory investment during a month, along with your annualized cost sales for the month. Do this at times when you think you're heavy with stock, at times when you think you're light, as well as at times when you think your stock is about right. Turnover ratios developed this way will help you identify approximate high and low ratios for your business or institution based on your judgment.

Let's say your ideal cost-of-sales-to-inventory ratio is about 4.3, either based on your experience and analysis *or* by comparing your cost-of-sales to inventory investment to other organizations in your industry. Once you've determined the target ratio appropriate for your firm, you may approximate the overall stock investment appropriate for your current or forecasted level of business, as indicated by the target ratio. Then you may find the indicated average inventory investment with the previous formula, now rearranged as shown below:

$$\text{Indicated Average Stock Investment} = \frac{\text{Cost-Of-Sales}}{\text{Desired Ratio}} = \frac{1,200,000}{4.3}$$

$$= \$279,070$$

Based on this determination, you decide to *reduce* your stock investment from $300,000 to $280,000, a reduction to approximately 93.3% of the original $300,000 investment. Before we go on to look at the other two ratios used to analyze stock levels, let's jump ahead slightly and look at *how* to cut our stock investment by 93.3% of its present $300,000 value.

Adjusting Stock Investment by Changing the Economic Order Quantity Index Number K. Continuing the same illustration, you have $300,000 invested in on-hand stock. You have decided to reduce stock level across the board to a level of $280,000 to keep it in balance with the current sales based on your target turnover ratio of 4.3. This amounts to 93.3% of the original investment.

You can accomplish this across-the-board proportional reduction in inventory investment by modifying the index number K, used with the EOQ formula, either up or down. For example, assume your K multiplier is 5.74, as we calculated in chapter 3. The adjusted index number if 5.34 (5.74 times 0.93). Use this new index number in your EOQ formula. Adjusting this number downward by 93.3% will proportionately reduce your stock investment by 93.3% of the original amount over a period of several months as you deplete on-hand stock and reorder. In practice, you may wish to round this number to one decimal place (5.3 in this example).

In the same way, you could increase stock investment by proportionately increasing the K multiplier. For example, you decide to increase your stock level 10% above its present level of $300,000 to $330,000 (or 110% of present level). Increase the index number K by the same amount. If K equals 5.74 originally, the new K to bring about the increased stock level is 6.31 (5.74 $\times$ 1.10 = 6.31).

By adjusting your K in this way, you can see you may make a proportionate adjustment to your average inventory for every item you stock. Over a period of several months, your average inventory level will increase or decrease by the same proportion that you increased or decreased the K multiplier.

Remember, adjusting the index number in this way is a fine-tuning procedure. It is not a substitute for estimating expected sales for each stock item and using the sales estimate in the EOQ formula. Normally rely on your estimated increased (or decreased) item sales figure to modify your order quantity and stock investment. Use the index number adjustment procedure as just described for *policy changes* up or down in stock investment, and then only gradually and in small increments to observe the effect.

Ratio of Sales to Average Inventory. A first cousin to the cost-of-sales-to-inventory ratio is the actual-sales- (at selling price) to-average-inventory ratio. Sales figures are often easier to get or estimate than cost-of-sales figures and therefore the sales-to-inventory-cost ratio is often more practical to use. Many businesses use the ratio of actual sales to inventory as an index of the appropriate stock level. Using the figures from the previous example, yearly sales are $2,000,000 and average stock is $300,000. The ratio of sales to average stock investment is:

$$\text{Ratio} = \frac{\text{Actual Sales}}{\text{Average Stock Investment}} = \frac{\$2,000,000}{\$\ 300,000} = 6.67$$

You may use sales-to-average-inventory ratio as an index of stock investment instead of cost-of-sales to average stock investment. (Your sales-to-average-stock ratio will always be higher than cost-of-sales-to-average-stock ratio.)

Just as you did with the cost-of-sales-to-stock-investment ratio, you may note from time to time your approximate inventory investment during a month and the annualized sales for the month. Do this at times when you're heavy with stock, and also at times when you're light on stock.

Let's say you find the correct sales-to-stock-investment ratio is about 7.1, based on experience or analysis, or by comparing your sales-to-stock-level ratio with those of other organizations in your industry.

When you've determined the appropriate target ratio, 7.1 in our example, you may approximate the appropriate overall stock investment for your level of business as indicated by this target ratio. You may then find the indicated average stock investment with the formula now rearranged as shown below:

$$\text{Indicated Average Inventory Investment} = \frac{\text{Actual Sales}}{\text{Desired Ratio}}$$

$$= \frac{\$2,000,000}{7.1}$$

$$= \$281,690$$

Based on this determination you decide to *reduce* your stock investment from $300,000 to $280,000, a reduction of 93.3% or the original $300,000 investment. Adjust your index number K, as previously discussed, to bring your stock investment down to the desired amount of $280,000.

Stock Investment as a Percent of Sales. Another method of assessing appropriate stock level is by viewing stock investment as a percent of sales (or as the equivalent decimal fraction):

$$\text{Stock Investment as a } percent \text{ of sales} = \frac{\text{Stock Investment}}{\text{Actual Sales}} \times 100$$

$$\text{Stock Investment as a } decimal\ fraction \text{ of sales} = \frac{\text{Stock Investment}}{\text{Actual Sales}}$$

You can see that stock investment as a percent of sales is the same as stock investment as a decimal fraction of sales, except that the first (percent of) is multiplied by 100 to form a percentage. You also can see that stock investment as a decimal fraction is the same as the previous ratio of sales to stock investment, except each ratio is upside down with respect to the other (that is, the reciprocal):

$$\text{Stock Investment as a decimal fraction of sales} = \frac{\text{Stock Investment}}{\text{Actual Sales}}$$

$$\text{Sales to Stock Investment} = \frac{\text{Actual Sales}}{\text{Stock Investment}}$$

Since each is the reciprocal of the other, either index is converted to the other by dividing the ratio into one.

A reason to use stock investment as a decimal fraction of sales (or the equivalent percent form) is that some trade associations collect financial figures for their members and publish a cost-of-doing-business survey. Often an inventory investment is reported by these associations as a percent of sales for reference by association members.

For example, let's assume your trade association reports the average member's inventory as a percent of sales is 13.5% (or, in decimal fraction form, 0.135). You may convert this ratio of stock investment to sales (as a decimal fraction) to the equivalent sales-to-stock-investment ratio of 7.4 by finding the reciprocal (1.000 ÷ 0.135 = 7.4).

Using the same figures we used in our previous example, your present stock investment is $300,000 with yearly sales of $2,000,000.

Your inventory as a decimal fraction of sales is:

$$\text{Stock Investment as a decimal fraction of sales} = \frac{\text{Stock Investment}}{\text{Yearly Sales}}$$

$$= \frac{\$\ 300,000}{2,000,000}$$

$$= 0.15$$

(or, as a percent, 15%).

You have decided that a more appropriate stock investment for the upcoming period is 14% of sales (or 0.14), based on your analysis of business conditions and other industry figures. You may therefore find the indicated average stock investment with this rearranged formula:

Stock Investment = (Yearly Sales)

X (Stock Investment as a Decimal Fraction)

Stock Investment = ($2,000,000) X (0.14)

Stock Investment = $280,000

Therefore, your new desired stock level of $280,000 is 93.3% of the previous level ($280,000 ÷ $300,000 = 0.933), and you will adjust your index number, K, to 0.933 of its former value as previously explained.

FINDING AMOUNT OF STOCK INVESTMENT

How do you know how much money you have tied up in inventory at any time? There are two basic methods. One method is to take a *physical inventory*. To obtain a physical inventory, count each item, multiply it by average unit cost, and then total the extended value of all stock items. This is a physical inventory because you physically count each stock item. Because of the work involved, a physical inventory is usually only done annually.

The other method is a *book inventory*. It's called book inventory because it's the inventory value accountants keep on your accounting books. You can find your book inventory value yourself at any time. Book inventory starts with the dollar value you obtained from your last physical inventory. Add to the amount of your last physical inventory amounts for stock you've purchased since the last physical inventory. Subtract amounts representing the cost of goods you've sold.

Cost of goods sold is approximated from your actual weekly or monthly net sales figures. You (or your accountant) can calculate your ratio of cost-of-goods sold to net sales based on your previous annual profit-and-loss statement. As an example, assume the cost of goods sold for last year was $80,000; and net sales were $135,000. Your ratio of cost-of-goods sold to net sales if 59% ($80,000 divided by $135,000).

Let's say you want to find your book inventory as of June 30, 1985. Your physical inventory on January 1, 1985, was $25,000. Here's a simple way you may arrive at the June 30 book inventory:

Step 1: Find Stock Available for Sale:

Beginning stock inventory Jan. 1, 1985	$25,000
Stock Purchases Jan. 1 to June 30	+ 40,000
Stock Available for sale	$65,000

Step 2: Deduct Cost of Goods Sold:

Cost of sales (Net sales × 59%) = ($65,000 × 0.59)

	- 38,350
Book Inventory June 30, 1985	$26,660

In summary, adding the cost of stock purchases and subtracting the cost of stock sold leaves you with what's left in stock, the book value of inventory. Get your accountant to show you how to do this if necessary.

The value of your book inventory should be reasonably close to the actual inventory value, but is subject to slight errors due to possible pilferage or counting errors (see chapter 14). You find the amount of the error the next time you compare your book inventory with physical inventory. At this time, your book-inventory value will either be less or more than the physical inventory value (book inventory will likely be greater than the physical inventory value since some loss is expected).

In this way you can keep a running total of book-inventory value yourself and at any time obtain your approximate ratio of annualized sales to inventory investment, or one of the other indexes shown. If you think this ratio is high (or low), you can adjust your stock investment down (or up) with the index number, K, used with the EOQ formula, as we've previously described.

13. Taxes and Your Inventory

In previous chapters we discussed fine tuning your stock levels for maximum profit. In this chapter we'll talk about how stock investment affects taxes you pay—the kinds of taxes and how taxes go up or down based on the value of your inventory. First we will discuss *property tax*, and, second, how inventory value affects your reported income, and therefore the *income tax* you pay.

PROPERTY TAX

Most cities and counties in the United States levy taxes against all property valued as of a given date, often January 1 each year. Property is taxed at its value, and as a result this tax is sometimes called by the latin name *ad valorem* tax (meaning at value). The words *ad valorem tax* and *property tax* are synonymous.

Property tax is based on business equipment you own like office furniture, counters, display racks, and so forth. However, much of the property many businesses own is in the form of inventory. Therefore for practical purposes, property tax often translates as *inventory tax*.

The city and county governments in which your business operates will decide how much tax will be charged each year per thousand dollars of property. Because it is a tax rate in terms of each thousand dollars of property value, the tax rate is called a *millage rate* or just *mil* (*mil* is the standard prefix meaning 1/1000th). Let's say the combined tax rate for the city and county government jurisdictions where your business is located is 23 mils, and you have an inventory of items worth $100,000 as of January 1. From the millage rate you know your property tax millage rate is $23 per thousand dollars of stock, or the total property tax for a stock investment of $100,000 is $2,300 ($23 per thousand times 100 thousand).

For the city and county to know how much to bill you for taxes, you or your accountant must file a property tax return declaring the value of all business property you own as of January 1 (or other valuation date possibly used in your locality). Your tax bill is based on this tax return. You or your accountant will also need to establish the value of inventory you have on hand as of that date by some reasonable method, either a physical inventory you obtain by counting each item of stock and extending the count by unit cost, or by a book inventory valuation, based on your records, as described shortly.

Since your tax is based on the value of your on-hand inventory as of January 1, clearly you don't want to have any excess stock on hand as of that date. If you do, the excess stock costs you $23 per thousand dollars of excess stock in taxes (using the example millage rate). If you've got $5,000 excess stock you pay an extra $115 in property taxes unnecessarily ($23 × 5). As a result, you want to hold down your inventory as of the date of property-tax valuation, within reason of course.

Some retail businesses use property taxes as the basis for an after-Christmas sale (both to have a reason for a "sale" as well as to actually reduce stock on hand).

INCOME TAX AND STOCK VALUE

The income tax you pay each year is based on your business's net profit. The value of your stock investment affects your net profit as reported on your income-tax return. To find your net profit from gross sales, deduct (1) any returns or allowances, (2) the cost of goods sold, and (3) all expenses.

The amount of stock investment comes into play when you figure your annual cost of goods sold (the accounting term *cost of goods sold* means the same as *cost of stock sold*).

You can't determine cost of goods sold simply by adding together all the bills you pay suppliers, because you don't know how much of any order you received from a supplier was actually sold or how much is still unsold (both the beginning and end of your accounting year). As a result, the following method is used to find the cost of goods sold:

Beginning inventory value,	
January 1	$ 25,000
Purchases during year	85,000
Stock available for sale	$110,000
Less:	
Ending inventory value,	
December 31	- $ 30,000
Equals:	
Cost of goods sold, January 1	
through December 31	$ 80,000

The use of this procedure assumes that since you had $110,000 worth of stock available for sale during the year, and you had $30,000 in stock at the end of the year, then the difference between these two represents the cost of stock you sold, $80,000, as the cost of goods sold in this example.

Usually the values of beginning and ending stock levels for a year are based on an actual count—that is, the count of stock that's there—a count of the physical inventory. The count is extended by each item's cost and its value computed. The value of inventory based on a physical count is considered a precise valuation, and the cost of goods sold computed by beginning and ending physical inventories as just explained is also considered precise. That is, both are precise if the method of valueing stock is fair and consistent. More about that in succeeding sections.

EFFECT OF STOCK VALUATION AND COST OF GOODS SOLD ON PROFIT REPORTED

Let's pause a moment and recognize the direct effect the ending inventory value has on your reported profit. It's important to know this because later we'll discuss how different methods of valuing inventory affect profit reported for tax purposes, and therefore the income tax you pay.

We just saw how the most recent December 31 inventory valuation ($30,000) was used to find cost of goods sold ($80,000). Cost of goods sold is used on your income and expense statement to determine gross profit, and of course affects your net profit:

	AMOUNT	PERCENT OF SALES
Sales	$135,000	100%
Cost of goods sold	80,000	59%
Gross profit	55,000	41%
Operating expense	45,000	33%
Net profit (before tax)	10,000	7%

Now let's make two different assumptions about your December 31 ending inventory valuation for the same stock items and as shown in the previous example:

Assumption 1: The ending value of inventory came out $5,000 more due to item cost increases, resulting in an ending inventory valuation of $35,000 instead of $30,000.

Assumption 2: The ending value of your inventory came out $5,000 less (due to lost stock, breakage, or similar reductions) and ending inventory is $25,000 instead of $30,000.

Let's now look at cost of goods sold under both assumptions:

	ASSUMPTION 1 (HIGH STOCK VALUE)	ASSUMPTION 2 (LOW STOCK VALUE)
Beginning inventory value, January 1	$ 25,000	$ 25,000
Purchases during year	85,000	85,000
Stock available for sale	$110,000	$110,000
Less:		
Ending inventory value, December 31	35,000	25,000
Equals:		
Cost of goods sold January 1 through December 31	$ 75,000	$ 85,000

You can see the two assumed ending inventory values have also changed the cost of goods sold to $75,000 and $85,000, respectively. Now let's plug these two cost-of-goods-sold figures into your income and expense like this:

	ASSUMPTION 1	ASSUMPTION 2
Sales	$135,000	$135,000
Cost of goods sold	75,000	85,000
Gross profit	60,000	50,000
Operating expense	45,000	45,000
Net profit	15,000	5,000
(Before tax)		

The significance of this is that the lower the value of your ending inventory, the higher is your calculated cost of sales, and the lower is your reported profit. Because income taxes are a percent of your reported profit, for reducing income taxes it is to your advantage to value ending inventories at a low value when you have valuation options, as will be described.

BOOK INVENTORY VALUATION

A physical count of inventory is a relatively costly task for many businesses and institutions. However, at other times of the year you may need an estimate of inventory value or the amount of the cost of goods sold for an interim financial statement. At these times you may estimate your inventory value based on a book inventory value.

This means instead of physically counting items you have in stock and extending the count of each item by its cost, you determine inventory value by your accounting records. Accounting records were originally kept in books, hence the origin of the term *book inventory value*, often shortened to just *book value*.

Two methods of determining book inventory value are: (1) If you have stock-status accounting records for each item in stock, extend the on-hand stock balance shown on your stock records by each item's cost; and (2) Estimate the cost of goods sold based on a known ratio of cost of goods sold to sales, and calculate the book inventory at the end of an accounting period based on the estimated cost of goods sold as described herein.

Extending Stock Balances from Stock-Status Accounting Records. This method applies only if stock-status accounting records are kept for all or most items in stock. The on-hand stock balances on the records are extended by item cost, just as if the item count were from an actual count. The total of these extended item values comprise the total stock value. This extension, when performed manually, can still represent considerable labor.

However, if stock-status accounting is performed on a computer, it is relatively easy to value stock quickly, based on book inventory counts in computer memory and item costs. As a result, this method is more convenient when stock records are computerized than when stock records are not. In both computerized and manual systems, a book value is subject to reporting errors that would be otherwise reported in a physical count of on-hand stock, for example items withdrawn from stock and not reported, breakage not recorded, and pilferage.

Estimating Cost of Goods Sold as a Ratio to Sales. This method of estimating book inventory value may be employed whether or not there are individual stock-status accounting records. Also, this method does not require that each individual on-hand balance shown on stock records be extended by item cost.

Referring back to the previous example of finding cost of goods sold based on bracketing physical inventories, we know the cost of goods sold last year is $80,000, based on the two physical inventories. Similarly we also know actual net sales during the same period last year, let's say $135,000. From these figures we also know the cost of goods sold is 59% of sales for last year ($30,000 ÷ $135,000).

During the current year, we can estimate cost of goods sold for monthly or quarterly profit-and-loss statements without taking a physical inventory by multiplying net sales by 0.59 to approximate the cost of goods sold. Based on this same approximation of cost of goods sold, we may estimate the value of inventory at June 30 of the following year (continuing the previous example into the next year) by the following calculation:

Beginning inventory, January 1	$30,000
(based on a physical inventory)	
Purchases January 1–June 30	40,000
Stock available for sale	$70,000
Less:	
Cost of goods sold January 1–June 30	−35,400
($60,000 sales times 59%)	
Equals:	
Ending inventory (book) June 30	$34,600

ADJUSTING COST OF SALES BY VALUING INVENTORY
TO MINIMIZE TAXES

For tax-accounting purposes, your beginning and ending stock may be valued using either of two costs. This is possible because your stock purchase cost trends up during times of rising prices. An item you bought a year ago now costs more. This item could be anything you stock (whenever you see the word *item*, substitute the name of a popular item you actually stock.) If you had a stock of a given item on hand both at the beginning and end of the year, for tax purposes you have the option of *reporting* the item stock value based on whether you've sold the stock of earlier-purchased less-costly items (and therefore have left a stock of the more costly, but otherwise same items, producing a higher-valued inventory), or you've sold the later-purchased more-costly items (and therefore have left a stock of less-costly items, producing a lower-valued inventory).

In the first case we assume the first items you received in were also the first ones you took out and sold—that is, "first in, first out." In the second case, we assumed the last items you received in were the first you took out and sold—that is, "last in, first out."

FIFO and LIFO are abbreviations for first-in-first-out and last-in-first out. These are accounting methods for valuing your inventory. These methods produce different period-ending stock values (ending inventory valuations) and in turn produce different cost-of-goods-sold figures. Consequently, they change your net profit (for tax purposes) up or down, as I've shown you previously.

LIFO, for example, is the accounting concept that assumes the last item you received in stock was the first one you took out and sold. During periods of rising prices you can therefore value a large amount of your inventory at the lower cost you paid for stock the previous year. It produces a lower-valued inventory than FIFO, a higher cost of sales, a lower reported profit, and therefore a lower income-tax liability. Alternately, FIFO means the first item you received in inventory is assumed to be the first one you took out and sold. FIFO has the opposite characteristics of LIFO.

Bear in mind that neither of these accounting methods has anything to do with how you actually handle stock on a day-to-day basis. These accounting techniques are for obtaining the most favorable tax treament for you. Therefore these accounting valuations are made on your accounting books, and don't affect day-to-day stock-management decisions. The sole end effect is whether you pay more or less income tax, and other than this, doesn't have any other day-to-day effect. If you decide to use the LIFO method to reduce your tax liability, you'll likely need the assistance of an accountant or tax advisor to employ it.

And while you wish to report the smallest possible profit for tax purposes (and the LIFO method enables you to do so legitimately), you correspondingly wish to report accurate profits for management information, and possibly for obtaining bank loans or other purposes. In this event you may want to use the higher (and more accurate) inventory value (perhaps based on the average cost of stock items, rather than their highest cost).

14. Stock Security

This chapter shows you how to detect if stock losses are occurring in your business or institution, and describes methods by which you can prevent and control unauthorized stock losses. Studies have shown that between 20% and 30% of all business failures are due to customer and employee theft, and the amount of such theft in the United States amounts to billions of dollars each year. As a result, you will want to make sure adequate controls exist to prevent stock loss, and to signal such a possibility if it does occur.

DETECTING STOCK LOSSES

Comparison of Physical and Book Inventory Valuations. The most direct indicator of unauthorized stock loss at the item level is comparison of actual item counts (based on a physical inventory count) against the same on-hand stock levels appearing on your written stock records. Losses of stock will therefore appear as count discrepancies. This ability is another reason for using written stock records, particularly for high volume and costly items.

If a computer system is used for stock-status accounting, such a comparison between physical counts and on-hand stock levels is relatively easy to implement with the already-established computer system. Since inventory valuation by extending counts by unit cost will likely be performed on the computer, it is relatively simple to add a direct comparison of the count data that is the most accurate indicator of stock loss.

However, without a computer stock-control system, such an item-by-item count comparison may be relatively costly to perform for all items. In this event, you may elect to compare physical inventory counts against records of on-hand balances for only key items. Additionally, you may elect to make irregular spot checks of key item counts at times other than when a regular physical inventory count is normally made.

High Cost of Goods Sold as an Indicator of Stock Loss. If stock is regularly removed from your stockroom, supply area, or other location without proper authorization, it will have the effect of increasing the cost of goods sold on your periodic financial statement, over that which you would ordinarily experience. Therefore, high cost of goods sold is an indicator of possible stock theft. For example, assume a part of your annual income and expense statement looks like this:

Description	Amount	% of Sales
Sales	$1,000,000	100
Cost of Goods Sold	$ 600,000	60
Gross Profit	$ 400,000	40

You may determine whether or not your cost of goods sold is high by comparing your cost of goods sold as a percent of your sales (60% in the example above) with reported industry averages (for example, assume the average for your industry is 50%). You may also make the same comparison with other branches of your same business, with other comparable firms, or you may notice your cost of goods sold is trending up.

If the average cost of goods sold for your industry is 50%, what may actually be occurring in your business or institution is the following:

Description	Amount	% of Sales	
Sales	$1,000,000	100	
Cost of Goods Actually Sold	500,000	50	
Cost of Goods Stolen	100,000	10	} 60%
Gross Profit	400,000	40	

For making this comparison, the cost of goods sold should be obtained by your accountant based on two bracketing physical inventories (instead of book inventory values). Additionally, the same valuation method should be used by your accountant for both bracketing inventories (check with your accountant on the best method for consistent valuation). Regardless of the method of inventory valuation, the following is an example of how cost of goods (presumed) sold is normally calculated:

*1. Beginning inventory, January 1 (from physical inventory)	$550,000
2. Stock purchases, January 1–December 31 (from purchase records)	200,000
3. Stock available for sale (line 1 plus line 2)	750,000
*4. Ending physical inventory, December 31 (from physical inventory)	150,000
5. Cost of goods (presumed) sold (line 3 minus line 4)	600,000
* Bracketing physical inventories based on item count and cost extension.	

Because the bracketing physical inventory method is a standard way of calculating cost of goods sold for your income and expense statement, it should provide a reasonably accurate account of the cost of goods sold. However, unless you detect an abnormally high cost of goods sold, as described previously, this method of calculating goods (presumed) sold can mask the following possible condition:

1. Beginning inventory, January 1 (from physical inventory)	$550,000
2. Stock purchases, January 1–December 31 (from purchase records)	200,000
3. Stock available for sale (line 1 plus line 2)	750,000
4. Ending physical inventory, December 31 (from physical inventory)	150,000

5. a. Cost of goods Actually Sold $500,000
   b. Cost of goods lost and not sold   100,000
   c. Cost of Goods reported sold $600,000

Limitations of Method. Although cost of goods sold is useful as a stock-loss indicator, there are several limitations of which you should be aware. Differences in cost of goods sold as an indicator works (1) if you make no substantial changes in your item-pricing policy during the time of trend comparison, and (2) if you do not change the method of valuing your inventory.

When comparing your cost of goods sold as a percent of sales with industry averages, your prices must be approximately the same as industry average prices. If your prices are lower than the industry average, your cost of goods sold as a percentage of sales will naturally be higher.

Nevertheless, if your cost of goods sold is higher than the industry averages, or is trending higher, you should consider if unauthorized stock loss is a possibility and find if stock loss is actually the reason for your high cost of goods sold.

PREVENTING STOCK LOSSES

Although it is desirable to have a method of detecting stock losses as described previously, loss detection occurs after the fact. You must also consider controls to prevent stock losses before they occur. Naturally, any system of controls carries an administrative cost to implement and continue. First decide if the cost of a given method of stock-loss prevention is worth the expected cost of preventing the actual stock loss.

If you do decide to implement systems to prevent stock losses, here are some of the methods you will want to consider for such a system:

1. *Written stock receiving reports.* You will need stock receiving reports if you maintain a written stock-status accounting system. However, even if you do not maintain a written stock-status accounting system, you may wish to install a written receiving report system anyhow, so that you can effectively compare the

amounts shipped and received by your supplier with the amount you initially ordered. This is a good procedure to insure that the amount received coincides with that ordered before issuing a check in payment. For these and other reasons, written receiving reports are desirable.

2. *Written issue records* (Stock issued is charged to an invoice, rung up on a cash register, charged to a work order, or charged to a retail department). These methods insure that stock issues are accounted for and no stock is removed from your stockroom or warehouse without an appropriate record (unless it is removed without authorization, circumventing the issue records system).

3. *Limiting access to stockroom and providing physical security.* You must decide whether or not unlimited access by all employees to your stockroom is necessary or not. If it is not essential, limit access to the stockroom to designated authorized employees, and prevent entry to the stockroom by anyone not specifically authorized. Additionally, consider whether or not physical security, such as door locks, wire fences, or other physical restrictions, should be added to the stockroom area to prevent access except by authorized persons.

4. *Security of on-hand stock balance records.* It is desirable to insure that on-hand stock balance records cannot be changed by persons other than those authorized to work with them to cover up a corresponding theft from the stockroom. If this occurred, on-hand records would coincide with the on-hand stock balance after a theft occurred, and detection would be more difficult. Therefore, consider restricting access to stock-on-hand balance records, possibly locking them after normal business hours.

5. *Prepare written procedures for handling stock.* As the size of your business or institution grows, it will be necessary to establish more structured procedures for handling stock. At some point, it will be desirable for you to prepare written stockroom procedures so that all persons will know and understand what is expected of them in handling stock.

6. *Assign specific responsibilities to an employee for stockroom management.* Rather than permitting all employees to enter and use the stockroom, you may wish to structure the organization by

assigning an employee primary responsibility for stockroom management, operation, and physical security.

7. *Assign separate responsibility to an employee for stock-status accounting records, and update these records according to stock receipts and issues.* It is necessary for you to assign a separate and correspondingly reliable person to this job so that the actual disbursements to and from inventory and the accounting for these disbursements are separate responsibilities. For example, do not assign stock-status accounting responsibilities to the same person who is responsible for operating the stockroom.

15. Use of Computers and Programmable Calculators for Inventory Cost Cutting

Computers have three separate but related primary functions for improving stock management. The first is help in making the buying decisions for each item: when to buy, and how much to buy, under varying suppliers' programs and deals. The second is for stock-status accounting. And the third is for providing exception reports and other special information. Let's look at each function and the computer alternatives.

CALCULATING WHEN TO BUY AND HOW MUCH TO BUY

In chapters 2 through 8 we discussed the procedure for calculating the economic order quantity and the reorder point under several practical conditions. In all of these examples a simple four-function pocket calculator or desktop printing calculator helps in working out the figures. Of even more help is automatic computation of economic order quantities and reorder points, along with best quantity discount brackets.

You should know that it isn't necessary to have a stock-status accounting system on a computer to get automatically calculated economic order quantities or reorder points for each item you stock.

You may calculate economic order quantities and reorder points by the following types of computing devices:

1. Programmable pocket calculator (or pocket computer).
2. Mini or microcomputer.
3. Computer-prepared printed buying guide by a large computer system or an outside computer service.

Programmable Calculator or Pocket Computer. Several programmable calculators or pocket computers representative of small, inexpensive machines capable of automatically calculating economic order quantities and reorder points are shown in figures 15-1(a) and 15-1(b). Included in this illustration is the Hewlett-Packard HP 41C programmable calculator and the Texas Instruments TI 59 programmable calculator.

Figure 15-2 is a printed tape using the Texas Instruments TI 59 programmable calculator (showing the user prompting) for economic order quantity. Figure 15-3 shows the printout from a TI 59 for reorder point calculations.

Programs for these pocket-sized calculators and computers can be developed to meet your own special needs, and standardized programs are available from equipment manufacturers.

Figure 15-1(A). The Hewlett-Packard HP-41C programmable calculator. Right photograph shows optional printer and optical wand. (*Hewlett-Packard*)

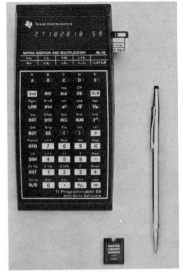 

Figure 15-1(B). The Texas Instruments TI 59 programmable calculator. Right photograph shows optional printer. (*Texas Instruments*)

```
          EOQ

SALES OR USE/WK?
         25.
HOLDING COST %?
         25.
ORDERING COST?
         4.00
UNIT COST?
         25.00
-------------------
ORDER QTY-
         41.        *
AVG STK INVMNT-
         509.90     *
-------------------
```

Figure 15-2. Printout of automatic calculation of economic order quantity performed by the TI 59 programmable calculator.

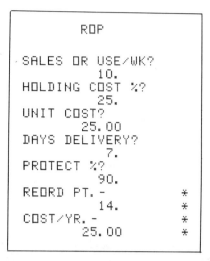

Figure 15-3. Printout of automatic calculation of reorder point performed by TI 59 programmable calculator.

Manufacturer supplied programs for Hewlett-Packard calculators are available from:

> Hewlett-Packard Users' Library
> Hewlett Packard Company
> 1000 N.E. Circle Blvd.
> Corvallis OR 973330

Programs for the Texas Instruments TI 59 calculators are available from:

> Professional Program Exchange
> Texas Instruments, Inc.
> P.O. Box 109
> Lubbock TX 99408

Additionally, TI 59 calculator programs for stock management are included in the book:

> *Using Programmable Calculators for Business*
> by C. Louis Hohenstein (John Wiley & Sons, 1981).*

*Available from Delta Business Publications, P.O. Box 7307, Atlanta, Georgia 30357.

Mini and Microcomputers. Mini and microcomputers are a development of space-age technology permitting small business computers to shrink to hi-fi stereo size. The same calculations for how much to buy and when to buy, described above with programmable calculators, may also be performed on any mini or microcomputer, like the Radio Shack TRS 80 microcomputer shown in Figure 15-4. The results are typically displayed on a video monitor or printed, as you desire.

Notice that it is possible for you to use a programmable calculator or computer along with a manually operated stock-status accounting system. In other words, it is not necessary for you to computerize stock-status accounting to obtain automatic calculation of reorder points and economic order quantities.

Computer-prepared printed buying guide prepared by a large computer or an outside computer service. The inventory management guide shown in Figure 10.5, as an example, can be prepared from basic existing data of item sales and unit cost. It's not necessary for you to have an existing computer stock-status accounting system to develop this

Figure 15-4. Mirocomputers are capable of performing stock status accounting when used with disk files. (*Radio Shack*)

printed buying guide. Also, an outside computer service can program and run this buying guide for you.

The buying guide lists stock-management information you need for each item. Figure 10-5 shows four stock items on one page. The entire printed buying guide has numerous pages, depending on the number of items stocked.

Item description is underlined for ease of location at the top of the applicable information for each product. Look at the item titled *#2 cotton tape* $\frac{3}{4}$ X *007*, second from the top, which we'll use as an example in describing the printed buying guide information. Item name is printed on both left and right sides for easy location and reference.

Below the item name are two sections of separate information. The first contains lines numbered 1 through 13. These lines show current information on each item, which we'll discuss line by line.

The second section printed below the 13 numbered lines is a table of precalculated economic order quantities and reorder points for each item at different levels of sales or use based on estimates of sales or use expected during a coming year. We'll also discuss this table in more detail.

Now I'll describe the first section, containing the 13 numbered lines of management data, line by line:

1. *Item Code.* This is the code number used in computer systems to identify the product (labeled in this example *PROD CODE*). If you are presently using a computer system for sales analysis (either through a computer service or in-house system), you will already have an item or product code. If not, you will need to assign item codes to your stock items. See chapter 10.
2. *Standard Unit.* This is the standard unit of measure for describing quantity for this product, like case, each, reel, package, etc. In this case, "RL" is an abbreviation for *reel*.
3. *Net Cost.* Purchase cost of the product (in this example) is shown. It's printed to show the current cost used in subsequent order quantity calculations.
4. *Annual Usage.* This is the sales (or use) for the previous year from a separate item sales analysis. Annual sales shows the relative activity of the item for the previous year in units (as op-

posed to the annual cost of sales below, which shows annual activity in dollars). If month-by-month sales data for the product is available, a computer forecast of the trend of sales can also be made, though it's not included on this report.

5. *Cost of Sales.* This shows the relative activity of the items, in dollars, for the previous year. It is computed by multiplying net cost (item 3) by annual usage (item 4). Also, the cost of sales for each item is accumulated by the computer to obtain a grand total for all items as a check against the cost of sales determined through other accounting methods for use on financial statements.

6. *Average Inventory Investment.* This is the average amount of money invested in inventory for this product ($104 in this example). Average inventory investment equals half the economic order quantity multiplied by item cost. In this example, it is $\frac{1}{2}$ times 669 times $0.31, equaling $104, to the nearest dollar. (The effect of safety stock on average inventory investment is considered negligible in this example and disregarded in figuring average stock investment.)

7. *Current economic order quantity.* Based on the known annual sales (line 4) and net cost (line 3), economic order quantity is calculated using the standard formula. The K value used in this example is 5.5. The economic order quantity that results is 669 (reels of tape).

8. *Number of replenishment cycles.* This is how many times the product will be ordered during the year based on the sales given in line 4 and the computed economic order quantity, and is shown on line 7. In this example, it's 6.9 times for the year, or about every 53 days.

9. *Weeks lead time.* Based on the buyer's estimate, four weeks is the current lead time for this item between the time stock is found low, and the time a new order is received. Reorder lead time is printed on the report to show the time used for calculating cycle stock and calculating safety stock, and in case the buyer wants to change the estimate because of more recent lead-time experience.

10. *Protection Factor.* The stockout protection factor of 1.85 is used in the safety stock calculation (line 13). This factor pro-

vides about 96% insurance against running out of stock during a reorder cycle.

11. *Safety Stock Cost.* The annual insurance premium, so to speak, this firm pays to get 96% insurance against running out of stock during the reorder cycle is $2.17. This amount is the annual *holding* cost for the 35 reels of safety stock shown in line 13. Safety stock is calculated by multiplying holding cost rate (20% for this firm) times safety stock (35 reels) times net cost ($0.31 per reel).

12. *Cycle Stock.* Cycle stock is the amount of stock used or sold during the lead time, based on sales (line 4) and lead-time estimate (line 9). Cycle stock plus calculated safety stock determines the reorder point (sometimes also called *minimum*).

13. *Safety Stock.* In addition to the 353 reels of tape normally sold or used during the four weeks delivery time, 35 reels of tape is added for protection against a stockout. This amount is calculated to provide 96% stockout protection during the replenishment cycle. It's calculated by multiplying 1.85 times the square root of cycle stock (1.85 × 353). The reorder point for this product is then the sum of cycle stock (353) plus safety stock (35), totalling 388 reels at the indicated annual sales.

All of these lines of information comprise base data for this item. The person responsible for ordering, however, is interested only in how much to order and when to order. That is, the manager wants to know the economic order quantity (how much) and the reorder point (when), based on the current sales (or use) level. The table below the lines of base information for each item (showing reorder points and economic order quantities) provides answers to how much and when to order for a range of sales levels.

The table is shown in four sections across the page under the thirteen items of base information. In each of the four sections, there are four columns of information:

1. Sales per month (labeled *Q/Mo.*).
2. Sales per year equivalent to the indicated monthly sales (labeled *Q/Year*).

3. The economic order quantity for the indicated sales level (labeled *EOQ*).
4. The reorder point for the indicated level (labeled *ROP*).

Economic order quantities and reorder points are calculated for a range of sales levels reasonably expected to occur during the coming year. The availability of a range of sales levels eliminates the need for the buyer to calculate individual economic order quantities and reorder points or to access a computer terminal since they appear directly on the printed report.

For each item stocked, the range of sales listed is from 10% *less* than annual sales during the previous year, to 50% *more*, at the end of the table. Therefore, for this example, the table begins at 4,125 reels sold per year (90% of last year's annual sales of $4,583 reels), and ends at 6,875 (150% of last year's annual sales 4,583 reels).

The sales/use levels between these extremes are equally spaced. There are 12 total entries in the tables. The interval for each entry is then (automatically) obtained by finding the difference between the end of the table (6,875 reels) and the beginning (4,125), a difference of 2,750. Since there will be 11 table entries above the table bottom of 4,125 reels, this difference is divided by 11 and produces a table increment of 250 reels. You can see, therefore, that each table entry is incremented by 250 reels each time to obtain the maximum table entry of 6,875 reels. At each sales increment listed, the computer calculates the corresponding economic order quantity and reorder point.

Since it's sometimes easier to think of sales in terms of monthly sales instead of annual sales, monthly sales is found by dividing annual sales level ($Q/Year$) by 12 and printing the equivalent monthly sales under the column heading Q/Mo.

In practice, when a reorder is indicated, the buyer checks the level of current monthly sales (or use), finds the economic order quantity in the table, and changes the reorder point for his next when-to-buy signal on the manual stock-status accounting records, if sales have changed from the previous level.

With this buying guide, stock-management decisions are made easier without the need for manual calculation or computer inquiry. The report can be run by an outside computer service or an owned computer system. All that is required is a knowlege of the previous year's sales (or use) level of each item, item description, and item code, along with cost information. In the event that sales (or use) is out of the range of the table, along with the base information already shown, a pocket calculator will give quick answers. If you wish to set up a report such as this, here are suggested steps:

1. Assign an item code to each of your stock items.
2. Accumulate the base input information you will need for each item: net cost, previous year's annual sales, desired stockout protection level, and inventory order quantity index number.
3. Decide on the format of the report you wish to use.
4. Turn this information over to your in-house computer center for production, or call in several outside computer services, describe the report you wish, and ask for quotations for them to run it.

COMPUTERIZED STOCK STATUS ACCOUNTING

In chapter 10 we looked at several typical written stock-status accounting systems. Stock-status accounting is also one of the most practical jobs for computers. Many existing programs are available to account for in-and-out inventory transactions, and then compute the current on-hand balance. The calculation to add and subtract stock receipts and issues is relatively simple. However, the amount of data the computer must store can be quite large (one computer record for each item in stock). Therefore, a relatively large computer memory is necessary. Frequently the memory used for storing inventory data is the magnetic disk, like a phono record, except the disk surface is magnetic and information is magnetically recorded or erased as necessary.

One characteristic of disk memory is virtually instantaneous access time to find a stock record. Because of the size of the required memory and the desirability of fast access time to stock records, a micro or minicomputer like that shown in the upper right of Figure 15-4 as an example, is often used for stock-status accounting.

On-line and Batch Systems. Two types of computer processing systems are (1) batch systems, and (2) on-line systems. A *batch* system means all in-and-out stock transaction data is gathered together and entered into the computer all at once as a batch. Periodically, weekly perhaps, a stock-status report is prepared showing on-hand inventory. Typically, batch stock-status accounting systems are used when the user is remote from the computer doing the processing; for example, when an outside computer service is used. Batch systems are used less frequently than on-line systems because of the value of having instantaneous access to stock records, as is possible with on-line stock-status accounting systems.

An *on-line* system is one in which inventory records may be updated at any time, even as they occur when invoicing. And correspondingly, on-hand stock levels are available at any time because the file containing the inventory status is always "on-line." On-line computer systems are used more frequently for stock management. Typically, a user purchases (or leases) a mini or microcomputer, along with the necessary program, and uses it at the office location where normal administrative and management work is performed. On-line systems for stock-status accounting may be used when the central computer is located remotely, but some type of computer communications link, like a telephone line-coupled computer terminal must be used.

STOCK-STATUS ACCOUNTING BY ON-LINE COMPUTER

Numerous computers of differing size and capacity are available for business use. Correspondingly, numerous programs are available for stock-status accounting. We will look at highlights of a typical stock-status accounting system and some representative reports.

Almost all current computer systems store stock records on a magnetic disk. Disks containing data are inserted to the disk drive, analagous to a record player. Two separate disk drives are desirable in a stock-status accounting system, one for storing programs and the other for the actual file of stock information. Each item you stock, therefore, will have a master record on the disk containing all information for that stock item. The typical data contained in a master record is shown in Figure 15-5. This information may be displayed on a video monitor, or (if your computer has a printer) printed at your discretion.

```
 1. VENDOR CODE (3):            AC
 2. PART NUMBER (12):           44
 3. PRODUCT CODE (1):           A
 4. DESCRIPTION (15):           SPARK PLUG
 5. COST PER PACK:                  0.25
 6. PRICE PER PACK:                 1.31
 7. SUB VENDOR CODE (3):        AC
 8. SUB PART NUMBER (12):       A49C
 9. QUANTITY ON HAND:             20
10. QUANTITY ON ORDER:           56
11. QUANTITY ON BACK-ORDER:      56
12. QUANTITY PER PACK:            8
13. REORDER LEVEL QUANTITY:       5
14. QUANTITY SOLD THIS MONTH:    32
15. QUANTITY SOLD YEAR TO DATE:  32
16. BIN LOCATION (3):          A45

DO YOU WISH TO DISPLAY ANOTHER RECORD (Y/N):
```

Figure 15-5. Typical master file information of a microcomputer. This master file data is often displayed on a video monitor.

Computer Reports and Visual Display of Stock Information. The results of the computer processing of on-hand quantity is also delivered either as a printed report, or visually on a video monitor. A problem with printed stock-status accounting reports is they must be updated and reprinted periodically, otherwise the stock condition will change and the original report will be out of date. On the other hand, printed reports are often useful because only one printer is required, and multiple report copies may be delivered to numerous different people.

Video monitors overcome some of the problems of printed reports because the monitor will display the exact on-hand balance, along with other stock information, at the exact moment of the inquiry. Video monitors are typically used with on-line systems. A problem with multiple video monitors, when several users need access to stock information at different locations, is their expense. If only one centralized desk for stock-status inquiry is all that's required, there's no problem. However, if numerous people at different locations must have access to stock-status information, then the number of video monitors (or other computer terminal performing the same function) can be a large cost factor of the data processing system. These decisions are elements of a data processing system configuration, and often a data processing system designer can help you make these decisions when you consider using a computer stock-status accounting system.

Entering Stock Transaction Data. The computer will do all of the work of adding and subtracting stock issued and received, and figuring the new on-hand balance of each item in stock once it's given the in-and-out transaction data for each item.

However, it is necessary to enter this in-and-out data to the computer. Quantities shipped or received are keyed on a keyboard by stock item number. Figure 15-6 shows a typical video display for adding a new item received in inventory.

Make sure you know or approximate the amount of time involved to enter this essential information before you install your computer system. The computer will not eliminate this data entry labor unless some type of automatic data entry system is used.

Automatic data entry systems use point-of-scale recorders attached to cash registers, or bar-code readers. These devices are not essential for stock-status accounting systems, but rather eliminate the labor

```
******************        INVENTORY SYSTEM - ORDERING ********************
*                                                                       *
*                                                                       *
*                                                                       *
*       1. VENDOR CODE (3):        AC                                    *
*                                                                       *
*       2. PART NUMBER (12):       44                                    *
*                                                                       *
*       3. DESCRIPTION (15):       SPARK PLUG                            *
*                                                                       *
*----------------------------------------------------------------------*
*       4. ENTER QUANTITY ORDERED:     5                                 *
*----------------------------------------------------------------------*
*       5. QUANTITY ON HAND:          20          20                     *
*                                                                       *
*       6. QUANTITY ON ORDER:         56          61                     *
*                                                                       *
*       7. QUANTITY ON BACK-ORDER:    56          56                     *
*                                                                       *
*                                                                       *
*                                                                       *
*       IS THE ABOVE DATA CORRECT (Y/N):     ?                           *
*                                                                       *
*************************************************************************
```

Figure 15-6. Typical display of a microcomputer inventory file for an item.

PHYSICAL INVENTORY WORKSHEET

VEN	PART NUMBER	DESCRIPTION	BIN LOC	PHYSICAL COUNT
YOA	215-009	BUSHING 3/4ID	P08	-------
YOA	103-095	AXLE	P13	-------
AC	A49C	AIR FILTER	T12	-------
WAL	21282	MUFFLER	T13	-------
YOA	104-095	AIR FILTER	T13	-------
EDI	N-135	DRILL SET 13PC	T14	-------
WAL	21000	MUFFLER 75 CHEV	T18	-------
WAL	21124	MUFFLER FORIGN	T19	-------
CHP	15678	GAS FILTER	T20	-------
EDI	N-865	TUBING CUTTER	T21	-------
EDI	N-173	IGN PLIERS 5"	T65	-------

PHYSICAL INVENTORY WORKSHEET

ON HAND	VEN	PART NUMBER	DESCRIPTION	(+)	(-)
4	YOA	215-009	BUSHING 3/4ID	-------	-------
1	YOA	103-095	AXLE	-------	-------
71	AC	A49C	AIR FILTER	-------	-------
13	WAL	21282	MUFFLER	-------	-------
21	YOA	104-095	AIR FILTER	-------	-------
-11	EDI	N-135	DRILL SET 13PC	-------	-------
-213	WAL	21000	MUFFLER 75 CHEV	-------	-------
1005	WAL	21124	MUFFLER FORIGN	-------	-------
0	CHP	15678	GAS FILTER	-------	-------
22	EDI	N-865	TUBING CUTTER	-------	-------
-95	EDI	N-173	IGN PLIERS 5"	-------	-------

Figure 15-7. Typical physical inventory worksheet printed as a by-product of a microcomputer inventory stock status accounting system.

otherwise required for manual key entry of stock transaction data. Additionally, some computer systems automatically update inventory records as a part of an automated invoicing procedure, as described in a subsequent section of this chapter.

COMPUTER-PREPARED EXCEPTION REPORTS AND OTHER SPECIAL INFORMATION

Computerized stock-status accounting systems allow you to automatically prepare a variety of special reports and status indicators. For example, some of these reports are (1) expedite lists, (2) back-order level reports, (3) sales or use analysis, (4) sales or use projections, and (5) physical inventory extensions.

As examples, Figure 15-7 illustrates a computer-prepared physical inventory worksheet of items listed in bin-number sequence in preparation for taking a physical inventory count. On-hand quantity physically counted is entered into the computer by the item number, and the count is extended by cost. Each line extension of inventory value is summarized to find the total physical inventory valuation.

Computer Systems for Order Entry, Invoicing, Accounts Receivable, and Stock-Status Accounting. Thus far we have discussed stock-status accounting systems as a freestanding and separate business function. However, the largest portion of the information regarding stock issues for wholesale distributors and many retail firms as well, originates with an invoice. As a result, it is possible and economically beneficial to use a computer for an integrated system for order entry, invoicing, accounts receivable, and stock-status accounting.

In addition to the stock-status accounting functions already previously described, an integrated ordering, accounts receivable, and stock-status accounting system works this way. Items ordered by customers are entered to the computer terminal, which prints invoices and maintains customer accounts receivable records. Often, monthly statements are printed, as well as an aged-accounts receivable analysis. As a by-product of order entry, the stock level of items ordered by each customer are automatically adjusted when the invoice is written. Packing lists and picking tickets are also printed to enable fast location of items in a customer's order. Additionally, sales analysis and other special reports can be developed.

Index